Learning RHEL Networking

Gain Linux administration skills by learning new
networking concepts in Red Hat Enterprise Linux 7

Andrew Mallett

[PACKT] open source *
PUBLISHING   community experience distilled

BIRMINGHAM - MUMBAI

Learning RHEL Networking

First published: June 2015

Production reference: 1170615

Published by Packt Publishing Ltd.
Livery Place
35 Livery Street
Birmingham B3 2PB, UK.

ISBN 978-1-78528-783-1

www.packtpub.com

Credits

Author
Andrew Mallett

Reviewers
Shichao An
Moinak Ghosh
Alexey Maksimov
Ranjith Rajaram
John Willis

Commissioning Editor
Nadeem Bagban

Acquisition Editor
Harsha Bharwani

Content Development Editor
Nikhil Potdukhe

Technical Editor
Parag Topre

Copy Editor
Relin Hedly

Project Coordinator
Vijay Kushlani

Proofreader
Safis Editing

Indexer
Monica Ajmera Mehta

Production Coordinator
Arvindkumar Gupta

Cover Work
Arvindkumar Gupta

About the Author

Andrew Mallett has been working in the IT industry since 1986. He has worked with Linux technologies since the release of the original Red Hat Linux 7 in 1999. Andrew not only possesses Linux skills and certifications, but also consults and teaches Linux and other technologies. He has written books on Linux on Citrix, which were published by Packt Publishing. Andrew has also been an active participant and works as a volunteer sysop. He is a SUSE Certified Linux Instructor, which enables him to help, support, and develop the official Novell SUSE curriculum worldwide.

Andrew currently works for his own company. He can be found on Twitter at `http://theurbanpenguin.com` and `@theurbanpenguin`. His published video courses on Linux can be found at `http://www.pluralsight.com`.

I live with my family in the UK. This year, I will celebrate 25 years of togetherness with my wife and friend, Joan, who has helped me sail through good and bad times. This book is dedicated to Joan and the 25 years of love she has selflessly provided.

About the Reviewers

Shichao An is a Red Hat Certified Engineer (RHCE). He uses Fedora as his desktop operating system. Shichao received his master's degree in computer science from the New York University. Currently, he works as a system administrator and focuses on managing Amazon EC2 servers and containerizes applications with Docker. Shichao is enthusiastic about open source and is active on GitHub, where he hosts some small projects and shares his learning roadmaps.

Alexey Maksimov is an IT professional raised in Russia. He has been living in New Zealand since 2008. He holds a diploma in mathematics and specializes in systems programming. During his extensive 15-year-long career, Alexey has gained broad infrastructure support experience from top notch enterprise-grade environments, such as Vodafone (New Zealand) and Mobile Telesystems (Russia).

Alexey's main area of interest is Oracle database administration. However, his skills also include impressive hands-on knowledge of networks and a range of UNIX-based systems, including Red Hat Linux, Oracle Linux, and Oracle Solaris, backed by industry certifications.

Alexey can be reached on LinkedIn at `http://linkedin.com/in/newrnz/` or on his personal website at `http://newr.co.nz/`.

His healthy mix of skills enable him to speak to other professionals in their language, understand and solve their challenges, collaborate effectively, and see the big picture beyond the fence of his job description, delivering a tremendous value to his employer. He has also worked as a professional IT trainer, which is very important if you are writing or reviewing books.

Ranjith Rajaram is employed as a senior technical account manager at a leading open source Enterprise Linux company.

He started his career providing support to web hosting companies and managing servers remotely. Ranjith has also provided technical support to their end customers. Early in his career, he worked on Linux, Unix, and FreeBSD platforms.

For the past 12 years, he has been continuously learning something new. This is what he likes and admires about technical support. As a mark of respect to all his fellow technical support engineers, he has included "developing software is humane but supporting them is divine" in his e-mail signature.

At his current organization, he is involved in implementing, installing, and troubleshooting Linux environment networks. Apart from this, he is also an active contributor to the Linux container space, especially using Docker-formatted containers.

www.PacktPub.com

Support files, eBooks, discount offers, and more

For support files and downloads related to your book, please visit www.PacktPub.com.

Did you know that Packt offers eBook versions of every book published, with PDF and ePub files available? You can upgrade to the eBook version at www.PacktPub.com and as a print book customer, you are entitled to a discount on the eBook copy. Get in touch with us at service@packtpub.com for more details.

At www.PacktPub.com, you can also read a collection of free technical articles, sign up for a range of free newsletters and receive exclusive discounts and offers on Packt books and eBooks.

https://www2.packtpub.com/books/subscription/packtlib

Do you need instant solutions to your IT questions? PacktLib is Packt's online digital book library. Here, you can search, access, and read Packt's entire library of books.

Why subscribe?

- Fully searchable across every book published by Packt
- Copy and paste, print, and bookmark content
- On demand and accessible via a web browser

Free access for Packt account holders

If you have an account with Packt at www.PacktPub.com, you can use this to access PacktLib today and view 9 entirely free books. Simply use your login credentials for immediate access.

Table of Contents

Preface

Welcome to *Learning RHEL Networking*. My name is *Andrew Mallett* and I will offer you expert guidance and tuition that will provide you with the skills to tame this powerful and popular Linux distribution. We will work with Red Hat Enterprise Linux 7.1. This latest release offers many improvements and is more likely to be the next version. The movement to the new system, the service management of systemd and the ecosystem that spawns from it offers so much new for administrators to absorb.

Writing about an Enterprise Linux distribution is important as we see the increase in the number of organizations deploying Linux. As a result, we require knowledgeable professionals to manage these systems. The Linux Foundation with Dice, a specialist recruitment company, surveyed many large organizations and found the following results:

- 93 percent of the organizations polled were looking to employ Linux professionals
- 91 percent of hiring managers reported that they found it difficult to find skilled Linux administrators
- As a side note to this, it was additionally noted that salaries for Linux professionals had increased by 9 percent during the last 12 months.

With such confidence in Linux coming from so many organizations, the focus of this book has to be commercially driven for me and you. We want you to be able to improve your career prospects as well as your Linux knowledge.

Enterprise Linux distributions, such as CentOS, Red Hat, Debian, and SUSE Enterprise Linux, do not deploy the latest and greatest bleeding-edge technology that you may find on home or enthusiast-oriented distributions, such as Fedora or openSUSE. Rather, they allow these to be development platforms to hone and perfect the software before migrating it to an enterprise a few months or even years later. Enterprise Linux has to be dependable, reliable, resilient, and supportable by the organization deploying it and the backend support coming from the community or paid support teams. By definition, the latest in software development does not lend itself well to this; these are the latest development, and knowledge of these developments and best practices will take time to evolve and develop.

Although the book will focus on RHEL, you may equally use Fedora 21 or CentOS; either of these releases will be able to provide you with a compatible platform, where we can work through many examples that are provided in the book.

What this book covers

Chapter 1, *Introducing Enterprise Linux 7*, helps you understand how enterprise-level Linux differs from other bleeding-edge distributions and the relationship between Red Hat, CentOS, and Fedora. This short chapter gives you a great understanding of RHEL and helps you learn RHEL 7 on your choice of platform.

Chapter 2, *Configuring Network Settings*, discusses how to configure your network settings and how Red Hat allows you to set the IP address configuration on your host.

Chapter 3, *Configuring Key Network Services*, helps your RHEL host with a network address. This chapter teaches you how to add some command networking services and how to configure NTP, DNS, DHCP, and SMTP, time, name resolution, IP address assignment, and e-mails.

Chapter 4, *Implementing iSCSI SANs*, discovers RHEL 7. It offers a new kernel-based module to implement network-based storage. This chapter teaches you how to deploy iSCSI targets and connect from an RHEL client.

Chapter 5, *Implementing btrfs*, takes a look at *Better FS*. Having volume management built-in the filesystem allows easy storage management and is a common basis for sharing your filesystem on a network.

Chapter 6, *File Sharing with NFS*, explains NFS, a de facto Unix file sharing service, which still maintains its importance in the Enterprise Linux market. This chapter covers how to use NFSv4 and compares it with V3 so that you can appreciate its easier firewall management feature among many other new features.

Chapter 7, Implementing Windows Shares with Samba 4, covers instances where RHEL can provide services on a network and the client-side workstation will have Windows OS installed at their end. This requires RHEL to support these Windows clients. File and print services can be supplied through the Samba 4 service on RHEL 7.

Chapter 8, Integrating RHEL 7 into Microsoft Active Directory Domains, explores the fact that many enterprise organizations have already set up Identity Services and are run with Microsoft's Active Directory. It makes sense that these existing domain accounts should be used to access resources on the RHEL 7 server. The RHEL server can join the domain server and become a member server that allows you to share single sign-on to shared resources hosted on the Linux system.

Chapter 9, Deploying the Apache HTTPD Server, deploys a web server that can be important for your network. This may be to provision web access to an intranet or external access to the Internet. Many administrators use the Apache web server to provide access to local software repositories and install sources, so the importance of this service cannot be overlooked.

Chapter 10, Securing the System with SELinux, provides insights on the fact that with more and more systems connecting to the Internet, the vulnerability of your network facing services is increasing exponentially. SELinux has been included on RHEL since release 4, but very often, we read blogs that suggest that SELinux should be disabled. This chapter teaches you how to deploy systems with SELinux effectively.

Chapter 11, Network Security with firewalld, provides insights on how to effectively use firewalls on your RHEL 7 system with the latest command-line tool, the firewalld service, and the firewall-cmd command. Throughout the book, we have presented practical uses of the latest firewall and how to open the required ports and services. The book concludes with details of this service and how to effectively secure your server with firewalld.

What you need for this book

The book uses Red Hat Enterprise Linux 7.1. Evaluations can be downloaded directly from Red Hat at `https://access.redhat.com/downloads`.

Should you not want to use RHEL, you may use Fedora 21 or CentOS 7 from:

- Fedora can be downloaded from `https://getfedora.org/en/workstation/download/`
- CentOS 7 can be downloaded from `http://www.centos.org/download/`

Who this book is for

This book is designed for Linux administrators or those wanting to learn Linux administration from scratch.

Conventions

In this book, you will find a number of styles of text that distinguish between different kinds of information. Here are some examples of these styles, and an explanation of their meaning.

Code words in text are shown as follows: "The /etc/issue content will be displayed before the logon prompt."

A block of code is set as follows:

```
zone "tup.local." IN {
  type master;
  file "named.tup";
};
```

Any command-line input or output is written as follows:

```
$ sudo vi /etc/named.conf
```

 Warnings or important notes appear in a box like this.

 Tips and tricks appear like this.

Reader feedback

Feedback from our readers is always welcome. Let us know what you think about this book—what you liked or may have disliked. Reader feedback is important for us to develop titles that you really get the most out of.

To send us general feedback, simply send an e-mail to feedback@packtpub.com, and mention the book title through the subject of your message.

If there is a topic that you have expertise in and you are interested in either writing or contributing to a book, see our author guide on www.packtpub.com/authors.

Customer support

Now that you are the proud owner of a Packt book, we have a number of things to help you to get the most from your purchase.

Errata

Although we have taken every care to ensure the accuracy of our content, mistakes do happen. If you find a mistake in one of our books—maybe a mistake in the text or the code—we would be grateful if you would report this to us. By doing so, you can save other readers from frustration and help us improve subsequent versions of this book. If you find any errata, please report them by visiting http://www.packtpub. com/support, selecting your book, clicking on the **errata submission form** link, and entering the details of your errata. Once your errata are verified, your submission will be accepted and the errata will be uploaded to our website, or added to any list of existing errata, under the Errata section of that title.

Piracy

Piracy of copyright material on the Internet is an ongoing problem across all media. At Packt, we take the protection of our copyright and licenses very seriously. If you come across any illegal copies of our works, in any form, on the Internet, please provide us with the location address or website name immediately so that we can pursue a remedy.

Please contact us at copyright@packtpub.com with a link to the suspected pirated material.

We appreciate your help in protecting our authors, and our ability to bring you valuable content.

Questions

You can contact us at questions@packtpub.com if you are having a problem with any aspect of the book, and we will do our best to address it.

Introducing Enterprise Linux 7

Welcome to the world of enterprise-level Linux version 7. This was first introduced to us on June 9, 2014. Red Hat started its journey with Red Hat Enterprise Linux (RHEL) 7 with its beta release on December 11, 2013. This was followed by the next release candidate on April 23. Finally, as expected, the gold release reached the market on June 2014. Currently, at the time of writing this book, we have Update 1 in the beta release. During the course of this book, this is what we will use for demonstration purposes.

This chapter will help you understand why enterprise-level Linux differs from other bleeding edge distributions. It will also help you understand the relationship between Red Hat, CentOS, and Fedora. We also hope that this short chapter will give you a great understanding on how to use RHEL 7 on your hardware platform of choice. The topics for this chapter are broken down as follows:

- Red Hat Enterprise Linux
- CentOS
- Fedora
- Determining your distribution and version

Red Hat Enterprise Linux

When we think of Linux, more often than not, Red Hat will be a primary consideration; almost certainly, if we are working at a corporate level, Red Hat will become part of our estate. Reliability, predictability, and stability are words synonymous with this very profitable and successful organization. To give an idea of their recent success, the company's share price on the Nasdaq (RHT) in 2010 was less than $30. However, towards the end of 2014, their value hovered around $60.

Enterprise Linux is not likely to be on the bleeding edge. As an enterprise distribution, it has to be supportable and reliable. With the release of RHEL 7, we have seen the first use of version 3 of the Linux kernel within RHEL. The Linux kernel version 3 saw the light of day on July 22, 2011. So, we can say that enterprise Linux may be some 3-4 years behind the latest and greatest version.

In many respects, the reliability aspect takes precedence over the new kernel features that version 3 will offer. These features often relate to hardware and are not important because the enterprise-level hardware has to take a similar cautious approach within mission critical environments. We find that enterprise-level hardware has to be reliable and this leads to, perhaps, a lack of new untested features. Development of new hardware and drivers that reside in the kernel can be tested on smaller businesses and home users. These beta testers can go through the torment while the developments can be improved for our mission-critical servers. A blue chip enterprise company demands a level of support that goes beyond posting a technical query within a support forum and hoping that someone will see it and respond to it. Almost certainly, any financial organization will have to be able to prove their level of support for their systems. This is most easily achieved by presenting your support agreement or contract and the associated service level agreement or SLA. To this end, Red Hat is not free, but the payment is taken for support and not for the distribution purpose. The simplest level of support starts at around $350 (US dollars) per year.

Red Hat began with **Enterprise Linux** in 2002 with RHEL version 2.1. Initially, the support was provided for 10 years, but has been extended to 13 years with RHEL 7. This means that the support for RHEL 7 can extend to June 30, 2027. The current RHEL 7.1 beta version uses the Linux kernel 3.10.0-210 compared to 3.10.0-123 with the 7.0 release. Here, we see tiny increments in the kernel version indicative of the care taken in rolling out any version of RHEL. At the time of writing, the very latest Linux kernel available from maintainers (`https://www.kernel.org`) is version 3.18.1.

Red Hat products can be downloaded from `https://access.redhat.com/downloads`. You will need to create an account to be able to start an evaluation and download RHEL.

CentOS

CentOS (Community Enterprise Operating System) has been commonly used and totally free of charge as a Red Hat rebuild for many years. This is where Red Hat logos and branding are removed from the system and redistributed as "CentOS". This is not quite as bad as it may first seem. Red Hat uses the open source code and redistribution is totally within the remit of the **GPL (GNU Public License)** agreement. What you lose out on is support. So, you may well find CentOS more used within smaller business operations and academia (where external support is not as critical). Support for CentOS is available only through public forums. Of course, this means that there is no guaranteed service level available.

CentOS began its operation in 2004 and is now entering its second decade. The free of charge product it brings on the market replicates the same reliability and predictability of its Red Hat cousin. The relationship between Red Hat and CentOS was more formalized in January 2014. The governance panel at CentOS now includes Red Hat board members among their numbers.

CentOS does not release beta versions in the same way as Red Hat. This means that the latest version available from the CentOS stable is version 7.0. This will use the same kernel and version 3.10.0-123 as the RHEL 7.0 distribution. The close resemblance between CentOS and Red Hat often means that CentOS becomes a perfect study platform for those wishing to learn Red Hat and, perhaps, gain their certifications. This is certainly a very viable option and the same applies to studying this book. Although, we will be using RHEL 7.1 beta, if you want to use CentOS, this should be very similar and mostly compatible with CentOS 7.

As CentOS does not offer subscription support, this in turn affects the product life cycle. To obtain the entire 13 years of support that RHEL 7 offers, a RHEL customer will have to purchase extended support for the final 3 years coverage. This means that CentOS has repositories that will distribute updates for 10 years, resulting in the fact that CentOS 7 can continually be updated until June 2024. Not bad at all when you see it like this and all without financial cost.

You can download the latest version of CentOS without the need to create an account directly from `http://centos.org/download/`.

Fedora

We can say that Fedora is the home version of Red Hat. Although we have marked this as a home version, Fedora ships in a server version and it's your choice as to how and where you use Fedora. The support for newer laptops and the latest hardware is going to be far greater. This then often makes it a target for home users and enthusiasts. The current version is Fedora 21 and uses almost all the very latest kernel with version 3.17.4-301.

The other advantage of using Fedora, even if not in a production format, is that you become familiar with technologies. These technologies will become enterprise-ready at some point. In this way, you will learn as the product is developed. For example, RHEL 7 is based around Fedora 19 and 20. If you have been an enthusiastic Fedora champion, you will already be familiar with GRUB2, BTRFS, docker, and systemd (all of which debut in RHEL 7).

Support for Fedora is community-driven with software updates available for about 13 months from the initial product launch. For example, Fedora 21 will be supported for 1 month after the release of Fedora 23. The release dates are about every 6 months, which gives us an approximate support life of 13 months. This is often why Fedora (and similar distributions to Fedora) do not make it to the enterprise category because of such a short update life cycle.

For learning and home use, this is truly a great distribution. You can choose to download the workstation, server, or cloud version at `https://getfedora.org/`.

From a popularity perspective, Fedora is certainly there. The numbers of hits to the Fedora download page over the past twelve months rates Fedora as being the fourth most popular distribution. To support this data and to take a look at where we read this from, you may visit `http://www.distrowatch.com`.

Determining your distribution and version

If you are installing from scratch, then we hope that you are able to determine what you are actually installing. If you can't, then we have some issues we need to resolve before the installation. Often though, you may be faced with a machine that is preinstalled or a lab machine that you may have access to. An obvious first step to any faultfinding task will be to determine the actual OS and patch level that we will work on. We will now look at the many ways that exist to determine the flavor of Linux that you will use.

The /etc/system-release file

The `/etc/system-release` file is consistent across all Red Hat variants that we have discussed here. This can be simply read with the `cat` command, short for concatenate. As a matter of fact, on all three systems, this file is a symbolic link that provides a shortcut to the relevant file from the following list:

```
/etc/redhat-release
/etc/centos-release
/etc/fedora-release
```

However, reading the linked file does make sense as the `/etc/system-release` file will always be available on any of these flavors and points to the correct OS file. Running the following command on the demonstration RHEL 7.1 system reveals the following command:

```
$ cat /etc/system-release

Red Hat Enterprise Linux Server release 7.1 Beta (Maipo)
```

The /etc/issue file

A second method could be to read the login banner from a standard terminal on the physical box. These physical terminals can be `tty1` through to `tty6` if no graphical system is running on the device. However, if you are running a GUI on your desktop or server, then often `tty2` is the first command-line terminal. You can access this terminal from the GUI with the *CTRL + ALT + F2* key sequence. The `/etc/issue` content will be displayed before the logon prompt. The `/etc/issue` content needs to be read by the `/sbin/agetty` TTY program. We can concatenate the file, but it's not useful because it contains special escape characters. These characters are expanded by **agetty**. Looking at the file as plain text, we see the following command:

```
$ cat /etc/issue

\s
Kernel \r on an \m
```

The `\s` command will display the OS, the `\r` command will display the kernel version, and the `\m` command will display the machine type. On the RHEL 7.1 system, we will use this file as displayed when logging on from a terminal as:

```
Red Hat Enterprise Linux Server 7.1 (Maipo)
Kernel 3.10.0-210.el7.x86_64 on an x86_64
```

Using lsb_release

If there is one way to display the OS details that you are using, why should there not be three ways! As is typical with Linux, we can address this issue in many ways. A third way is to use the `lsb_release` command. This is generally not installed as part of the default installation. So, it needs to be added to your system (if this has not already been done).

Installing this software can be achieved using `yum`, but this needs to be run as the `root` user (administrator). So, either use `su -` to switch to the root account or use `sudo` if your account is set up as an administrator, as shown in the following code:

```
$ sudo yum install redhat-lsb-core
```

 If you are new to the Linux administration, then the next chapter will start with a quick lesson on how administrative rights are gained and managed within RHEL.

Despite the `redhat` element in the package name, this command can also be used on CentOS (if this is the system you are using for your journey to Enterprise 7 Linux). With the package installed, we will use the `lsb_release` command to identify the OS. On the system we use for this book, we can view the following output:

```
$ lsb_release -a
LSB Version:     :core-4.1-amd64:core-4.1-noarch
Distributor ID: RedHatEnterpriseServer
Description:     Red Hat Enterprise Linux Server release 7.1 Beta (Maipo)
Release:         7.1
Codename:        Maipo
```

If you are using Fedora, you can install the package using the following command:

```
$ sudo yum install redhat-lsb
```

The output is similar, but relates to the Fedora release, as shown in the following output from the Fedora 21 server:

```
$ lsb_release -a
LSB Version:      :core-4.1-amd64:core-4.1-noarch:cxx-4.1-amd64:cxx-
4.1-noarch:desktop-4.1-amd64:desktop-4.1-noarch:languages-4.1-
amd64:languages-4.1-noarch:printing-4.1-amd64:printing-4.1-noarch
Distributor ID: Fedora
Description:     Fedora release 21 (Twenty One)
Release:         21
Codename:        TwentyOne
```

Determining the kernel version

We have seen that the Linux kernel version may well be displayed with the **/etc/issue** file when logging on to a terminal. However, we can also easily display the version of the current kernel using the uname -r command. The kernel is the core of an OS and is maintained as open source software by the Linux Foundation. This command can be run as a standard user. On the RHEL 7.1 system, it displays the following information:

```
$ uname -r
3.10.0-210.el7.x86_64
```

Again, knowing the version of the Linux kernel is a great starting point in order to build a picture of the system for faultfinding and placing support calls.

Summary

By now, I am hoping that you have a better understanding of what you are going to need to follow through this book and how it will help you learn Red Hat Enterprise Linux 7 networking, be it on RHEL, CentOS, or Fedora. You will now be able to differentiate the benefits of each distribution and identify the version that you will work on.

In the next chapter, we will start looking at configuring networks on RHEL 7. Additionally, we will look at how to gain administrative rights using su or sudo and its benefits. This will be particularly useful for those new to Linux administration and those who are a little lost with running tasks as an administrator.

2
Configuring Network Settings

Sitting here feverishly typing away at the keyboard, I am reasonably hopeful that the title of this chapter may allude in some way to what we will cover. So, I am eager that it will not be too much of a shock when I reveal that we will discover how to configure networking on your RHEL 7 system in this chapter. However, breaking this down a little, we will look at a little more than just networking. Firstly, we will make sure that you are up to speed with how to gain administrative rights in Linux. Although, this has nothing to do with networking, gaining administrative rights becomes the ground for much of what we will do in the book. Once we have finished with the initial rights section, we will then quickly move on to investigate how networking is configured on RHEL 7. In this chapter, we will cover the following topics:

- Elevating privileges
- Using `ip` and `hostnamectl`
- NetworkManager and network scripts
- Interacting with NetworkManager
- Using the Control Center
- Using the `nmtui` menu
- Interacting with `nmcli`

Elevating privileges

As an administrator of the RHEL server or desktop system, there will be times when root access will be required. The root user or user ID 0 is the local administrator on the system. Although it's possible to log in to the system as a root user, as with most systems, it's preferred that root access is gained as required. There are two mechanisms that can be used:

- The substitute user or the su command
- Using the sudo command

First, we will look at the su command.

The su command

When a user issues the su command without specifying a username, they will be prompted for the root password. If authentication is successful, they will be presented with a root shell. The following are the valid mechanisms to gain root privileges with su:

- su -l: This presents a full login shell for root; all environment variables are set for root. The working directory of a user is changed to become the home directory of the root user, which is usually /root.

- su: This is the same as su -l.

- su: This presents a nonlogin shell, where the full profile or environment of the root user is not loaded. The result is that some variables—such as $USER—are not reset and the current directory remains unchanged. Although presented with the nonlogin shell, the correct root password is still required for authentication.

Using the su command is a simple way to gain rights. This may be a convenient option for an administrator. For a small environment, this may be acceptable; however, within an enterprise environment, this is not often viable because auditing is limited. It's possible to trace who used the su command to gain rights; this will be recorded in the /var/log/secure log file. As all activities from this point forward will be logged as root, we have no granularity to understand which administrator ran any particular command. The other big downside with this method is that the user will need to know the root password. This again is a big security issue and a complete no-no as far as I am concerned.

Although we want to use the su command, we can control who has access to su using **PAM (Pluggable Authentication Modules)** in conjunction with the wheel group. By adding users to the special administrative group: wheel, we can limit access to the su command to members of that group.

To add users to the wheel group, you will need to run # usermod -a -G wheel <username> as root user, where <username> is the login name of the account that should be added to the wheel group. The -a option is used to append a group to the user's current group membership list.

To ensure that only members of the wheel group use the su command, you must, as root, edit the /etc/pam.d/su PAM configuration file. Open the file in your desired text editor—such as vi or nano—and uncomment the following line by deleting the # character from the start of the line:

```
#auth required pam_wheel.so use_uid
```

With this change in effect, only members of the wheel administrative group will be able to use the su command in order to switch to another user ID.

Should you so wish, you can make a second change to the /etc/pam.d/su PAM file in order to ensure easy access to su for members of the wheel group. The recommendation for this file will be limited to systems—such as classroom or lab machines—where security is not an issue.

Edit the /etc/pam.d/su file and uncomment the following line by deleting the # character from the start of the line:

```
#auth sufficient pam_wheel.so trust use_uid
```

With this change in place, members of the wheel group are not required to authenticate with a password while using su; this is the default behavior of root.

> Both these PAM edits are consistent across Red Hat variants that we have discussed: RHEL 7, CentOS 7, and Fedora 21. Additionally, by default, the root user is part of the wheel group.

Delegating with the sudo command

In my opinion, using the sudo system is another approach and a more secure way of delegating administrative privileges. This system serves as a mechanism of preceding administrative commands with sudo and fine-grained delegation through the /etc/sudoers file.

Once users are trusted and tasks are delegated to them in the /etc/sudoers file, they can then run commands trusted to them using sudo. The basic command syntax is as follows:

```
$ sudo <command>
```

In the preceding example, <command> will be replaced by the administrative command normally reserved for root user, as shown in the following command:

```
$ sudo useradd bob
```

The command string listed previously allows a trusted user to create a new user account: bob. It will be normal for a user to be prompted for their password when a command with sudo is first run. The system defaults to cache their credentials for 5 minutes. In this way, should they need to run several commands as a root user using sudo over a short time period, they will be prompted just once for their password.

With sudo, we do not need to divulge the root user's password to our administrators or delegate a specific command or group of commands to individuals or groups.

To delegate rights for a user called sally to be able to run the useradd command along with the passwd command, an entry can be added to the /etc/sudoers file. We can also prevent sally from changing the root password within the same entry. This will be similar to the following command:

```
sally ALL=(root) /sbin/useradd, /bin/passwd , !/bin/passwd root
```

Editing should be implemented as root using the visudo command. In this way, changes are verified before they are saved (preventing corruption of the file). More detailed configuration examples can be obtained by consulting the man pages:

```
$ man sudoers
```

By default, with sudo, members of the wheel administrative group are permitted to run all commands without any additional administrative effort.

To elevate security in order to acquire the password of the user to be entered for each sudo command and overwrite the default timeout of 5 minutes, use visudo and add the following line to the /etc/sudoers file:

```
Default     timestamp_timeout=0
```

For the rest of the book, administrative commands will be run as a standard user and prefixed with the sudo command. The user will be a member of the wheel group. In this manner, we hope to set best practice with security at the heart of your thinking.

Using ip and hostnamectl

Many administrators on Linux have become used to using the `ifconfig` command in order to display and set IP addresses on Linux hosts. Although the `ifconfig` command is still valid, it's marked as obsolete in favor of the `ip` command. For Microsoft Windows administrators who move to Linux, the use of `ifconfig` becomes the obvious choice. As `ipconfig` closely resembles the Windows command line, I encourage you to learn the ongoing `ip` command and all that it has to offer. Using either the `ifconfig` or `ip` command on RHEL 7 will also introduce new, consistent device names. This may come as a little shock to those used to `/dev/eth0`.

Finally, we will look at something very new to RHEL using the `hostnamectl` command. This can be used to set the `hostname` for the current session and persistently in a single shot, rather than using the `hostname` command and editing the `/etc/hostname` file.

[handwritten: hostnamectl → sets hostname → Edits /etc/hostname]

Consistent naming for network devices

With the hardware that we have on servers and desktops, we now see far more use of multiport interface cards and **LOM (LAN on motherboard)** interfaces. If you rely on the more traditional `eth0` and `eth1` naming scheme, all this will lead to inconsistent network device naming.

Within RHEL 7 and the related family of similar distributions, `udev` supports a number of different naming schemes for network devices. This defaults to the assignment of fixed names based on firmware, topology, and location information returned from the device itself. In this way, the naming is related to the physical device itself and remains consistent and predictable even in the advent of failed hardware that is replaced. What we need to achieve is the avoidance of any possibility of the `eth0` device becoming `eth1` and vice versa. The disadvantage is that the name can be longer and less easily remembered. With reference to the RHEL 7.1 system that we will use throughout the course of this book, the single Ethernet interface on the VMWare hosted system is named as `eno16777736`.

The naming aspect is managed by `systemd`, the new initialization daemon, and supports the following naming schemes when detecting hardware during the boot phase:

[handwritten: onboard]

[handwritten: enoxxx]

- **Scheme 1:** This scheme specifies names that can incorporate firmware or the BIOS information returned from onboard devices. These names can take the form of `enoxxx` (letter o as in onboard). If this fails, the naming system falls back to scheme 2.

hotplg slot

ensxxx

- **Scheme 2:** This scheme specifies names that can incorporate firmware or the BIOS information returned from PCI Express slot cards. These names can take the form of ensxxx. If this fails, the naming system falls back to scheme 3.

enpxxx

PCI or usb

- **Scheme 3:** This scheme specifies names that can incorporate the physical location of the connector — such as the slot address — on the motherboard. These names can take the form of enpxxx. If this fails, the naming system falls back to scheme 5 (note that scheme 4 is optional).

- **Scheme 4:** This scheme identifies names based on the **MAC** (**Media Access Control**) address of the **NIC** (**Network Interface Card**) and selected by the administrator by setting the HWADDR (hardware address) attribute in the network configuration file. These names take the form of the name supplied within the interface configuration file's DEVICE attribute. For example, if you want to rename a LOM interface card from eno16777736 to internal, working as root, you will edit the /etc/sysconfig/network-scripts/ifcfg-eno16777736 file. You will be required to add the HWADDR attribute and edit the DEVICE attribute so that the file reads similar to the following extract:

```
HWADDR="00:0c:29:57:ef:c4" #Using the MAC address for your
NICDEVICE="internal"
```

ethø,

- **Scheme 5:** If all else fails, the naming system will fall back to the traditional kernel unpredictable naming scheme, such as eth0, eth1, and so on.

To summarize, each interface device will normally have a two character prefix. This denotes the protocol type of the NIC. The following list illustrates these prefixes:

- en: This denotes Ethernet
- wl: This denotes wireless LAN
- ww: This denotes Wide Area Wireless

The character that follows the prefix denotes the naming scheme used and the type of hardware detected, as shown in the following table:

Position 3 of device name	Description
o	This is the onboard device
s	This is the hot-plug slot
p	This is the PCI or USB device

eno onboard

ether NGT

Interface 2 = (en) ethernet
(address) p9 or PCI address p9 (bus 9)
and s0 for slot 0.
Chapter 2

You can get this also by doing

A real-life network device naming example

In order to show you the consistent network device naming system on a physical machine and a virtual machine we have been using so far, we will venture out to my Dell laptop that runs on the Fedora 21 workstation. This has a wired network card (which is not currently connected) and a wireless port (which is the active connection). Using the `ip address show` command, we can see two physical interfaces and the local or the `loopback` interface:

```
[andrew@boromir ~]$ ip a s
1: lo: <LOOPBACK,UP,LOWER_UP> mtu 65536 qdisc noqueue state UNKNOWN group default
    link/loopback 00:00:00:00:00:00 brd 00:00:00:00:00:00
    inet 127.0.0.1/8 scope host lo
       valid_lft forever preferred_lft forever
    inet6 ::1/128 scope host
       valid_lft forever preferred_lft forever
2: enp9s0: <NO-CARRIER,BROADCAST,MULTICAST,UP> mtu 1500 qdisc mq state DOWN group default qlen 1000
    link/ether 00:1c:23:4c:61:5d brd ff:ff:ff:ff:ff:ff
3: wlp12s0: <BROADCAST,MULTICAST,UP,LOWER_UP> mtu 1500 qdisc mq state UP group default qlen 1000
    link/ether 00:1c:bf:90:37:42 brd ff:ff:ff:ff:ff:ff
    inet 192.168.0.20/24 brd 192.168.0.255 scope global dynamic wlp12s0
       valid_lft 86160sec preferred_lft 86160sec
    inet6 fe80::21c:bfff:fe90:3742/64 scope link
       valid_lft forever preferred_lft forever
[andrew@boromir ~]$
```

When we look at device names and ignore the local interface: `lo`, we see interface 2 as `enp9s0` and interface 3 as `wlp12s0`.

For Interface 2:

- The wired Ethernet is `en`
- The PCI bus address is `p9`
- The slot number is `s0`

We can view this PCI device using the `lspci` command; the command and output is as follows:

```
$ lspci | grep 09:00.0
```

```
09:00.0 Ethernet controller: Broadcom Corporation NetXtreme BCM5755M
Gigabit Ethernet PCI Express (rev 02)
```

We can see this does relate to the physical device mentioned in the naming scheme (PCI Bus 9 and slot 0 in the Ethernet card).

For Interface 3:

- The wireless Ethernet is `wl`
- The PCI bus address is `p12`
- The slot number is `s0`

Again, using `lspci` and `grep`, we can see this device. The PCI bus (`12`) in hexadecimal appears as `0c` from the output of `lspci` because this uses hexadecimal and the device naming scheme uses decimal values:

```
$ lspci | grep 0c:00.0

0c:00.0 Network controller: Intel Corporation PRO/Wireless 3945ABG
[Golan] Network Connection (rev 02)
```

Disabling consistent network device naming

For simplicity, especially where you have a single interface, you may preferably use the traditional name (`eth0`). You may also have legacy software that requires this naming scheme. These legacy names can still be used, as you learned when using the naming scheme 4. Adding the `HWADDR` attribute to the network configuration file and either renaming the `/etc/syconfig/network-scripts/ifcfg-eth0` file or configuring the `DEVICE` name attribute with a value of `eth0` will help you achieve your goal.

To set this globally across the system for all interfaces, you will be required to use additional kernel parameters at boot time. This can be set via GRUB2 in the `/etc/default/grub` file. The `GRUB_CMDLINE_LINUX` line should be changed to the following code, appending the `biosdevname` and `net.ifname` command:

```
$ cat /etc/default/grub
```

```
[andrew@redhat7 ~]$ cat /etc/default/grub
GRUB_TIMEOUT=5
GRUB_DEFAULT=saved
GRUB_DISABLE_SUBMENU=true
GRUB_TERMINAL_OUTPUT="console"
GRUB_CMDLINE_LINUX="rd.lvm.lv=rhel/swap crashkernel=auto rd.lvm.lv=rhel/root rhgb quiet"
GRUB_DISABLE_RECOVERY="true"
[andrew@redhat7 ~]$
```

Once the file is edited and saved, we can update the GRUB2 configuration with the following command:

```
$ sudo grub2-mkconfig -o /boot/grub/grub.cfg
```

We then need to reboot our system to see that the view changes to interface names:

```
$ sudo shutdown -r now
```

> It's strongly recommended that you persevere with the consistent names and accept that this naming scheme addresses the inconsistent nature of device-naming that the traditional kernel names previously presented to administrators.

For the rest of this book, we will use the standard naming system associated with the single NIC on the RHEL 7.1 system, that is, `eno16777736`.

Using the ip command to display configurations

We started this chapter outlining with the fact that the preferred command to use to display and configure the IP address configuration from the command line on RHEL 7.1 is ip. The `ip` command is part of the `iproute` RPM package and replaces the now obsolete `ifconfig` command, which is part of the net-tools RPM. The `ifconfig` command is still installed, but `ip` is preferred.

We can display the IP address for all interfaces, using the `address show` option for the `ip` command. This can be implemented in one of the three ways, shown as follows:

- `$ ip address show`
- `$ ip a s`
- `$ ip a`

We start with the verbose use of options, where the full `address show` command is used. This can be abbreviated to `a s`, or as the default action is `show` for the address command, just use `ip a`. Extending this a little, we can display the IP address for just a single interface or a single protocol as follows:

```
$ ip a s eno16777736
$ ip -4 a s eno16777736
$ ip -6 a s eno16777736
```

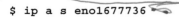

The following screenshot displays the command and output from the demonstration system when you view the IPv4 address for the configured NIC:

```
[andrew@redhat7 ~]$ ip -4 a s eno16777736
2: eno16777736: <BROADCAST,MULTICAST,UP,LOWER_UP> mtu 1500 qdisc pfifo_fast state UP qlen 1000
    inet 192.168.40.3/24 brd 192.168.40.255 scope global eno16777736
       valid_lft forever preferred_lft forever
[andrew@redhat7 ~]$
```

> The use of the dynamic term within the third line of the scope global dynamic eno16777766 output is indicative of an address assigned via **DHCP (Dynamic Host Control Protocol)**.

To view the transmission statistics for this same interface, we change to the link option, as shown in the following command line and output:

```
$ ip -s link show eno16777736
```

```
[andrew@redhat7 ~]$ ip -s link show eno16777736
2: eno16777736: <BROADCAST,MULTICAST,UP,LOWER_UP> mtu 1500 qdisc pfifo_fast state UP mode DEFAULT qlen 1000
    link/ether 00:0c:29:57:ef:c4 brd ff:ff:ff:ff:ff:ff
    RX: bytes  packets  errors  dropped overrun mcast
    33183      338      0       0       0       0
    TX: bytes  packets  errors  dropped carrier collsns
    15094      211      0       0       0       0
[andrew@redhat7 ~]$
```

We can already start to feel the flexibility associated with this command, but we are not restricted to just link and address as options. In the following commands, we first view the route table and then the **ARP (Address Resolution Protocol)** cache. Each command is shown in the verbose form and then short form. The shortened form is especially useful if you can't spell neighbor:

```
$ ip route show
$ ip r
$ ip neighbor show
$ ip n
```

> The ARP cache displays the MAC addresses of the devices that you have connected to that exist on the same network.

Using the ip command to implement configuration changes

As a stalwart at displaying the configuration information, the `ip` command is a dab hand at changing the IP address's dynamic configuration too, this time using `add` in place of `show`. For example, to add an additional IPv4 address to our interface, we will use the following command:

```
$ sudo ip address add 192.168.140.3/24 dev eno16777736
```

We can now view this information using the `show` command we looked at previously, as shown in the following command and output:

```
$ ip -4 a s eno16777736
```

```
[andrew@redhat7 ~]$ ip -4 a s eno16777736
2: eno16777736: <BROADCAST,MULTICAST,UP,LOWER_UP> mtu 1500 qdisc pfifo_fast state UP qlen 1000
    inet 192.168.40.3/24 brd 192.168.40.255 scope global eno16777736
       valid_lft forever preferred_lft forever
    inet 192.168.140.3/24 scope global eno16777736
       valid_lft forever preferred_lft forever
[andrew@redhat7 ~]$
```

When we look carefully at the output, we can see the DHCP address we had before and the additional address we have just applied. Although these settings have been added only for this session, on a restart of the network or interface, we will revert to the single DHCP assigned address.

To restart all interfaces using network services, we will use the following command:

```
$ sudo systemctl restart network.service
```

If we have more than one interface in the system and we are using the NetworkManager service, which is the default interface, we can stop and start a single interface using the following commands:

```
$ sudo nmcli dev disconnect eno16777736
$ sudo nmcli con up ifname eno16777736
```

 There will be much more information on the `nmcli` command later in this chapter.

So, although we can add IP addresses dynamically to our running system, if we want the change or changes to be permanent, then we need to add the configuration information to the configuration file.

Persisting network configuration changes

To change from the DHCP assigned address we are using on the demonstration RHEL 7.1 system, we will assign a static address in the network configuration file related to our /etc/sysconfig/network-scripts/ifcfg-eno16777736 interface. To edit the text file, you can use your favored text editor: vi or nano; here, we will use vi:

```
$ sudo vi /etc/sysconfig/network-scripts/ifcfg-eno16777736
```

After editing the file in the preceding command line, it should read similar to the following file content. Of course, with any pertinent information to your network being set as opposed to IP addresses, we use:

```
TYPE="Ethernet"
BOOTPROTO="none" #Change from dhcp to none
DEVICE="eno16777736" #use your device name
ONBOOT="yes"
PEERDNS="yes"
PEERROUTES="yes"
IPADDR="192.168.40.3" #use the IP Address that you want to assign
NETMASK="255.255.255.0" #Use the appropriate subnet mask
DNS1="192.168.40.2" #the address or your DNS server
GATEWAY="192.168.40.2" #the default gateway to use
DEFROUTE="yes"
IPV4_FAILURE_FATAL="no"
IPV6INIT="yes"
IPV6_AUTOCONF="yes"
IPV6_DEFROUTE="yes"
IPV6_FAILURE_FATAL="no"
NAME="eno16777736" #use your device name
UUID="980c9e81-f018-42ae-9272-1233873f9135" #use your device UUID
IPV6_PEERDNS="yes"
IPV6_PEERROUTES="yes"
IPV6_PRIVACY="no"
```

As always, take care when editing files. In reality, much of the file can stay as it is because we edit changes to just the following one line:

```
BOOTPROTO="none"
```

Add four new lines:

```
IPADDR="192.168.40.3" #use the IP Address that you want to assign
NETMASK="255.255.255.0" #Use the appropriate subnet mask
DNS1="192.168.40.2" #the address or your DNS server
GATEWAY="192.168.40.2" #the default gateway to use
```

With the changes made and saved, we need to refresh NetworkManager using the following command:

```
$ sudo nmcli connection reload
```

This will re-cache the network configuration files. With this done, we can stop and start the following interface:

```
$ sudo nmcli dev disconnect eno16777736
$ sudo nmcli con up ifname eno16777736
```

Alternatively, just restart the network service as we did before. This single command replaces three commands here. However, it disrupts all interfaces. So, the following command should only be used where we have a single interface:

```
$ sudo systemctl restart network.service
```

Now that we have a static IPv4 address configured for our interface, we will now see that we lose the keyword dynamic from the output from the ip address show command:

```
$ ip -4 a s eno16777736
```

We have now seen how we can successfully configure IPv4 settings from the command line and through configuration files. We will now move on to the final part of the network configuration: the hostname.

Configuring the RHEL 7 hostname with hostnamectl

With the advent of systemd on RHEL 7 and its derivatives, we have a brand new way to display and set the hostname using the hostnamectl command. The advantage of this tool is that the static name and the transient name can be configured in one step.

We will edit the /etc/hostname file and add the new static hostname. This is then read by the kernel at system startup and displayed as the transient hostname, which is often used as part of your BASH shell prompt. The transient hostname can be displayed and set using the hostname command. This was a two part process: using hostname to set the transient name maintained by the kernel and editing the /etc/hostname file to ensure that it persisted across reboots.

With RHEL 7, we have these two hostnames and a third hostname: the pretty name. The pretty name can display UTF-8 characters that allow you to embed spaces and apostrophes. The pretty name, when set, is stored in the /etc/machine-info file.

To display the configured hostname, the hostnamectl command can be used. The pretty name will only be displayed if the configured hostname contains characters that cannot make up part of the static hostname. In the same way, the /etc/machine-info file will only exist if the pretty name is used to store a name incompatible with the /etc/hostname file:

To display the hostname as a standard user, the following command can be issued:

$ hostnamectl

```
[andrew@redhat7 ~]$ hostnamectl
   Static hostname: redhat7.tup.com
   Pretty hostname: Red Hat 7.tup.com
        Icon name: computer
          Chassis: n/a
       Machine ID: eeec69a9c3d64634b3be4fc877d17cae
          Boot ID: 91034e304efb4138864a32d60a684acb
  Operating System: Red Hat Enterprise Linux Server 7.1 (Maipo)
      CPE OS Name: cpe:/o:redhat:enterprise_linux:7.1:beta:server
           Kernel: Linux 3.10.0-210.el7.x86_64
     Architecture: x86_64
[andrew@redhat7 ~]$ 
```

As spaces are used in the hostname, the **Pretty hostname** will show. The **Pretty** and the **Static** names relate to the /etc/machine-info and /etc/hostname file respectively and can be used in the following command:

$ cat /etc/machine-info /etc/hostname

The output for the preceding command line results in the following output:

```
PRETTY_HOSTNAME="Red Hat 7-1.tup.com"
redhat7-1.tup.com
```

To configure the hostname using `hostnamectl`, we use the `set-name` option, as shown in the following command. This command does not need to be prefaced as `sudo` if the user is a member of the `wheel` administrative group, but the user will be prompted for their password. These permissions are configured using the policy kit:

```
$ hostnamectl set-hostname "Red Hat 7.tup.com"
```

This will set all three names; to see the transient name, a new shell should be initiated by running the `bash` command. To set individual names, include the correct option to `hostnamectl` as follows:

```
--transient
--static
--pretty
```

Introduction to the Red Hat NetworkManager

The `NetworkManager` service has been a part of RHEL since version 6 and in its simplest form allows users to configure network configuration settings (such as joining Wi-Fi networks). Of course, this is really necessary when we consider laptop users with a Fedora or an RHEL laptop. This service extends well beyond the GUI and to server products installed with or without the X Server environment.

The `NetworkManager` service that ships with RHEL 7 is a dynamic network control and configuration daemon to keep network interfaces active while they remain available. As we have seen, the `NetworkManager` service not only maintains support for the traditional `ifcfg-` file type, but also extends this support to additional profiles. In this way, we can easily have a static IP address configuration for your laptop for different offices that you may visit, rather than relying on DHCP on each site.

Configuration of the NetworkManager service can be maintained via the GUI control center or from the nmtui command line menu. We have also seen that we can avoid the menu, enabling scripting events from the command line, using the nmcli command.

To query the status of the NetworkManager service, we can use the systemctl utility, as shown in the following command and the associated output screenshot:

```
$ sudo systemctl status NetworkManager.service
```

```
[andrew@redhat7 ~]$ sudo systemctl status NetworkManager.service
NetworkManager.service - Network Manager
   Loaded: loaded (/usr/lib/systemd/system/NetworkManager.service; enabled)
   Active: active (running) since Mon 2015-05-11 13:16:41 BST; 17min ago
 Main PID: 920 (NetworkManager)
   CGroup: /system.slice/NetworkManager.service
           ├─ 920 /usr/sbin/NetworkManager --no-daemon
           └─1021 /sbin/dhclient -d -q -sf /usr/libexec/nm-dhcp-helper -pf /var/run/dhclient-e...

May 11 13:16:47 redhat7.tup.com NetworkManager[920]: <info>  parsing /etc/sysconfig/network-.....
May 11 13:16:47 redhat7.tup.com NetworkManager[920]: <info>  parsing /etc/sysconfig/network-.....
May 11 13:16:47 redhat7.tup.com NetworkManager[920]: <info>  parsing /etc/sysconfig/network-.....
May 11 13:17:10 redhat7.tup.com NetworkManager[920]: <info>  use BlueZ version 4
May 11 13:17:13 redhat7.tup.com NetworkManager[920]: <info>  (eno33554992): Activation: Stag.....
May 11 13:17:13 redhat7.tup.com NetworkManager[920]: <info>  (eno16777736): Activation: Stag.....
May 11 13:17:13 redhat7.tup.com NetworkManager[920]: <info>  (eno33554992): Activation: Stag.....
May 11 13:17:13 redhat7.tup.com NetworkManager[920]: <info>  (eno33554992): Activation: Stag...e.
May 11 13:17:13 redhat7.tup.com NetworkManager[920]: <info>  (eno16777736): Activation: Stag.....
May 11 13:17:13 redhat7.tup.com NetworkManager[920]: <info>  (eno16777736): Activation: Stag...e.
Hint: Some lines were ellipsized, use -l to show in full.
[andrew@redhat7 ~]$ █
```

Users and administrators can interact with the NetworkManager service by using one of the following utilities:

- The GNOME notification area icon
- The GNOME network settings control center
- The nmtui menu
- The nmcli command-line tool

Interacting with the NetworkManager using the Control Center

If you are using RHEL, CentOS, or Fedora on a graphical environment, then with the GNOME control center, we can interact with the NetworkManger service. We can also access network settings from the notifications area icon. This can be seen in the following screenshot on the RHEL 7.1 system:

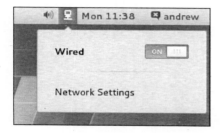

To access the same, but through the control center, we can use the **SUPER** key. In the search dialog box, we will enter `control network`, as seen in the following screenshot:

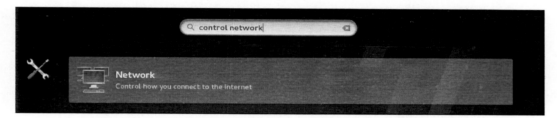

Once we have accessed **Network Settings**, it's possible to simply disable all wireless interfaces with the traditional **Airplane Mode**. In this way, you can be assured of not plummeting to your certain death during takeoff and landing and still enjoy your game of *Candy Crush Saga*.

On the left-hand side panel, we can view the current known interfaces and the **Network proxy** settings. Here, we can add web proxies if required. On the RHEL 7.1 system we are using in this book, we see two network interface groups on the left-hand side panel:

- **Wired**
- **Unknown**

In the graphic, the **Wired** interface represents my gigabit Ethernet card and the **Unknown** interface represents the local loopback connection. If your system includes a wireless card, you may well see **Wi-Fi** as an option too. While selecting the **Wired** interface from the left-hand side panel, the right-side panel will display your current network profiles. As we have only one profile, the name of this profile is not shown, but this will represent the default system profile we configured previously in this chapter: eno16777736.

From the bottom of the right-side panel, we can create additional profiles with the **Add Profile** button, whereas the gearwheel in the bottom right-side corner will allow you to alter the properties of the current profile. All of this can be seen in the following screenshot:

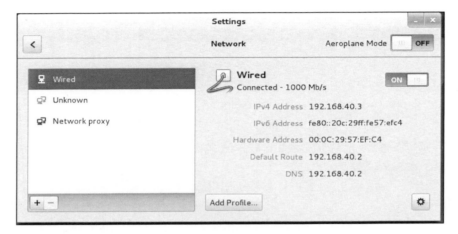

Adding a new profile with the Control Center

More useful for mobile systems, such as laptop devices and tablets, we may configure profiles to easily load network configuration information specific to the location where you use the device. For example, if you are using a laptop at home, you may have a specific static IP address set, whereas when at work, you may have a DHCP-assigned address. Profiles can handle this situation easily and effortlessly.

Using the **Add Profile** button from the Network Settings control center, we are presented with the **New Profile** dialog box. From the left-side panel, we can select an option from the following given options:

- **Security**
- **Identity**

- **IPv4**
- **IPv6**

We will create a new profile for DHCP for when at home; if you remember, we set a static IPv4 address earlier in the section using the traditional `ifcfg-` script located in the `/etc/sysconfig/network-scripts` directory. We will retain this setting and additionally allow ourselves to switch from the static address to DHCP and back as required.

Selecting the **Identity** option from the left-side panel, we will set **Name** to `home-DHCP`. From the drop-down list, choose **MAC Address** associated with the interface that we want to assign to this profile. Finally, we can deselect the checkbox to **Connect automatically** so that the default connection will still be the static assignment we chose earlier. We can manually select this profile as required. We can leave all the other settings as they are; this includes the automatic DHCP assignment of addresses for the **IPv4** and **IPv6** settings. Navigate to the bottom-right corner of the open dialog box and select the **Add** button to create a profile. The following screenshot shows the settings that we have chosen:

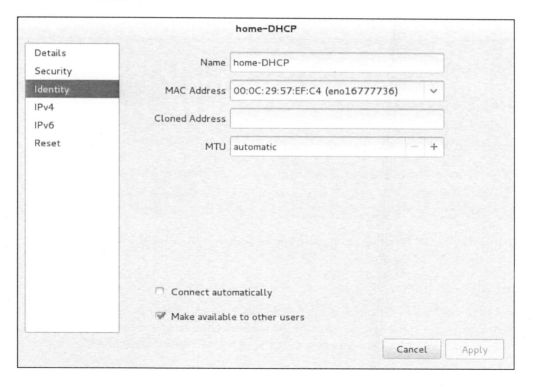

Having created the new profile, we can easily select between two profiles using the GNOME notification panel, which simplifies the transition between differing networks. In the following screenshot, we can see the currently selected **eno16777736** profile and how we can switch to the newly created **home-DHCP** profile:

We have now seen how we can set the network profile information using graphical tools on RHEL 7.1. For those running on RHEL or Fedora without the X server, we can easily manage the NetworkManager connection using the nmtui ncurses menu.

Interacting with the NetworkManager using nmtui

Just as with the GUI profile management within the GNOME control center, we can use the text user interface provided by the nmtui command. This is the traditional blue screen command-line menu provided by the ncurses system. If the command is not available on your system, then it can be installed using yum, as shown in the following command:

```
$ sudo yum install NetworkManager-tui
```

Once installed, the NetworkManager menu can be accessed using the following command:

```
$ sudo nmtui
```

If you are using PuTTY to connect to your server via SSH, then in order to ensure that the menu border show correctly, you should set the **Character set translation** option to **UTF-8**. This can be found in connection settings and **Window | Translation**.

The **NetworkManager** menu displayed on the RHEL 7.1 system used in this book looks clean, if a little simple, and is displayed in the following screenshot:

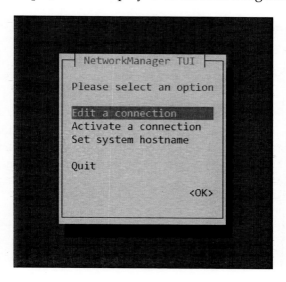

The nmtui command also offers shortcut wrappers to specific tasks within the menu. These take the form of the nmtui-edit, nmtui-connect, and nmtui-hostname commands. The first two commands are useful when you already know the name of the connection profile you want to activate or edit, whereas the last command sets the hostname system-wide.

To activate the home-DHCP profile we created previously, we will issue the following command:

```
$ nmtui-connect home-DHCP
```

This will effectively switch from the static IP address to the automatically allocated DHCP address. You should issue this command from the console and not remotely as you will lose your connection when the address is changed from static to DHCP.

This can also be used to connect to a new Wi-Fi SSID, should you be geeky enough to be using a command line-only version of Fedora while at Starbucks:

```
$ nmtui-connect Coffee-Shop-Wifi
```

To change the properties of the same connection profile, we will use the following command:

```
$ sudo nmtui-edit home-DHCP
```

This will open up the property page for the homeDHCP connection profile in readiness for editing purposes. To open the hostname menu page for editing purposes, you can use the following command:

```
$ sudo nmtui-hostname
```

Extreme interaction with NetworkManager using nmcli

For those who believe that the only true form of Linux is without the aid of menus, using solely the wisdom handed down to you through your Jedi parentage, we have the extreme sport of `nmcli`. Joking aside, working with the `NetworkManager` in this way, without interaction of menus, will allow you to make changes in scripts, which can then be implemented across many systems.

As a simple starter, we can use `nmcli` to scan for available Wi-Fi networks; the output should show you the Wi-Fi SSID and strength as follows:

```
$ nmcli device wifi list
```

This procedure is greatly simplified compared to the traditional command-line mechanism we have used before to display SSIDs with the `iw` command:

```
$ sudo iw wlp12s0 scan | grep SSID
        SSID: hobbit
        SSID: virginmedia1671684
        SSID: VM260970-2G
        SSID: virginmedia9066074
        SSID: Edinburgh2013
        SSID: TALKTALK-4C89F0
```

The process with `nmcli` is simplified for us, as the `NetworkManager` can use the configured `polkit` permissions. These permissions or actions (using the `polkit` language) are configured by the system administrator and are not meant to be changed by users. The policy file is located at the `/usr/share/polkit-1/actions/org.freedesktop.NetworkManager.policy` location.

We can use `nmcli` to display configured permissions with the following command:

```
$ nmcli general permissions
```

```
[andrew@redhat7 ~]$ nmcli general permissions
PERMISSION                                                    VALUE
org.freedesktop.NetworkManager.enable-disable-network         yes
org.freedesktop.NetworkManager.enable-disable-wifi            yes
org.freedesktop.NetworkManager.enable-disable-wwan            yes
org.freedesktop.NetworkManager.enable-disable-wimax           yes
org.freedesktop.NetworkManager.sleep-wake                     no
org.freedesktop.NetworkManager.network-control                yes
org.freedesktop.NetworkManager.wifi.share.protected           yes
org.freedesktop.NetworkManager.wifi.share.open                yes
org.freedesktop.NetworkManager.settings.modify.system         yes
org.freedesktop.NetworkManager.settings.modify.own            yes
org.freedesktop.NetworkManager.settings.modify.hostname       auth
[andrew@redhat7 ~]$ ▮
```

Should we want to be able to create a connection for the wired interface when it's up and available, we can do so with nmcli. This can also be easily scripted across many devices as and when required. Firstly, we create the connection profile, as shown in the following command and output:

```
$ sudo nmcli connection add con-name wired-home \
  ifname enp9s0 type ethernet ip4 192.168.0.8 gw4 192.168.0.1
```

```
        Connection 'wired-home' (e17cb6b7-685f-4cf2-9e8b-16cbfae1f73a)
successfully added.
```

This command is greatly simplified when you know the fact that tab completion is enabled even for subcommands and values—such as enp9s0—that we add as a value to ifname.

To complete the task, we need to add the DNS configuration to the connection profile, which we can affect with the use of the following command:

```
$ sudo nmcli connection modify wired-home ipv4.dns "192.168.0.3 8.8.8.8"
```

We can now display the properties with the following command:

```
$ nmcli -p connection show wired-home
```

The -p option used here is for the pretty output; for the terse output, -t may be implemented. Either way, the output is too verbose to show as part of the book.

We have now replicated creating a connection profile that we first saw when we started with the control center. We do not pretend that this is easy, but being able to script this presents a multitude of options not available with any form of interactive menu, be that the text menu from nmtui or the GUI from the control center.

Summary

In this chapter, we have really established a baseline of knowledge that we need to begin to understand networking on the RHEL 7 family. To begin with, you learned how to gain and manage privileges on RHEL using su and sudo. Further, we looked at how to restrict the use of su to members of the wheel group with PAM. We have also begun our administration in the way that we mean to continue, using sudo to manage administrative tasks rather than logging in as root or using su.

With the ground knowledge of rights set, we moved on to understand the new naming conventions of network devices on the Red Hat release. We learned why it's preferred, compared to traditional names before moving on to the network configuration.

To configure network interfaces, we can use traditional ifcfg- scripts and these are used by default. We can extend this to additional network profiles that are probably most useful with mobile devices—such as laptops—that connect to different network locations. We saw how these can be configured in many different ways from menus to raw command-line tools.

Next up, we will look at how to configure key network services, such as DNS, DHCP, and SMTP.

3

Configuring Key Network Services

It must be said that having a network is great and most fulfilling; however, the reasons for using that network must be challenged and understood. No one has a network for the sake of having a network, so we must bring services to our network to give it a purpose, meaning, and reason to exist.

Of course, there are many and varied services that we can add, many of which are covered during the course of this book. To begin with, we will look at the following topics:

- DNS (the name resolution)
- DHCP (the IP address assignment)
- NTP / PTP (time services)
- SMTP (e-mail)

Domain Name System

Domain Name System (**DNS**) servers help us to resolve friendly computer names, such as www.packtpub.com, to a less human-friendly IP address, such as 83.166.169.231. In this way, mere humans can access many computer systems by guessing the address or the DNS name. In the early days of UNIX computers, where access was limited to a few academic systems, hostnames were distributed by **Network Information Service** (**NIS**); a central computer maintained a single file that mapped hostnames to IP addresses. This file was then pushed out to client subscribers. Although this worked, it was clearly not scalable.

In 1988, the first release of the DNS server was developed by four graduates from UCB (the University of California, Berkeley). This software in now maintained by the **ISC (Internet Systems Consortium)**. Even today, it's still known as **Berkeley Internet Name Domain (BIND)**.

On Red Hat Enterprise Linux 7.1, the version of the DNS server or bind that is shipped is 9.9.4. Once installed, the version can be verified entering the following command:

```
$ named -V
```

The DNS server can be installed and run without changes to the configuration. In this mode, it will operate as a *Local Caching Only* server. When operated in this manner, a server can resolve names on the Internet, but it does not host any of its own records. Additionally, in a setup without configuration changes, only localhost can query the server. In its simplest form, a caching-only server is still useful, but you will want to at least open the access control list to allow queries from your own network for it to be useful. In this way, computers on a local network can resolve names from a local server. Only the single server needs access to the Internet for name resolution, decreasing the Internet footprint of the organization.

Installing and configuring a Caching Only DNS server

To begin with, we will install the `bind` package on our system and configure it to resolve names for hosts on the local network. There is little to do here other than a simple change to the configuration file, but it will get us started.

To install `bind` from console, enter the following command:

```
$ sudo yum install bind
```

With the package installed, we will now need to edit the `/etc/named.conf` configuration file:

```
$ sudo vi /etc/named.conf
```

We will edit three existing lines as follows:

- `listen-on port 53 { 127.0.0.1; };` changes to the following:
  `listen-on port 53 { any; };`

- `listen-on-v6 port 53 { ::1; };` changes to the following:
  `listen-on-v6 port 53 { none; };`

- `allow-query { localhost; };` changes to the following:
  `allow-query { localhost; 192.168.40.0/24; };`

The changes that we have made are explained here:

- Allows the DNS server to listen on all IPv4 interfaces
- Disallow the DNS server to listen on IPv6, unless you need it to listen on IPv6
- Allows queries from my local network
- Adjusts the address range to match your network and the subnet mask

With the changes in place, we will be able to save them. We can test the changes before we start the server. To do so, we will use the following command:

```
$ sudo named-checkconf
```

The output should be silent. The only output will occur if there are errors in the configuration. If you prefer an output, then you can make use of the -p option:

```
$ sudo named-checkconf -p
```

Using this option, we will be presented with configuration options as they are interpreted by the service. If there are errors, we will only see errors and not the configuration.

We can now start and enable the DNS service with the systemctl command; the order in which commands are executed is not important:

```
$ sudo systemctl start named
$ sudo systemctl enable named
```

For the purpose of these labs, we will not run the firewall at present. You can check this on your system using the following command:

```
$ sudo systemctl status firewalld
```

If it's running, then either stop the firewall if it's not required or enable the DNS traffic on UDP and the TCP port 53 to pass into the system. To stop and disable the firewall, use the following command:

```
$ sudo systemctl stop firewalld
$ sudo systemctl disable firewalld
```

From the local system, we can test the name resolution using our DNS server; we will use the IP address of our server to prove that it's accessible from the network, rather than just from the localhost alias. You can use the same command and make sure that the @address at the end of the sequence points to the address of your server:

```
$ dig www.packtpub.com @192.168.40.3
```

[Here, use the IP address of your DNS server in place of the address we use.]

You should now see the **ANSWER** section in your output, detailing the address of the Packt server.

If you have another system on the same network, you can use the identical command to verify that it does indeed work for any host on your network.

At this stage, we will have a working DNS configured in the caching-only mode.

Configuring clients to use this server

When we were using the `dig` command before to test our DNS lookups, we had hardcoded the name server that we used, ignoring the client configuration. Traditionally, the client configuration file was `/etc/resolv.conf`. We can still use this, but more often in more modern Linux systems, this is overwritten by the NetworkManager service, which will read the name server from the interface configuration. In this way, we can use different DNS servers for different connection profiles. Of course, DNS will work with other operating systems as well, including your Microsoft Windows desktops and Apple iPhones. Very often, the DNS server list is handed out to the **DHCP** service (**Dynamic Host Configuration Protocol**), affecting the configuration across all DHCP clients. We will look at DHCP a little later in this chapter.

On RHEL 7.1, we can use the following command to display an active connection:

```
$ nmcli con show active
```

My active connection shows `eno16777736`; this is the same system that we worked with in the *Chapter 2, Configuring Network Settings,* where we looked at the consistent network device name that we find on modern Linux systems.

We can modify DNS servers for this configuration using the `nmcli` command:

```
$ sudo nmcli con modify eno16777736 ipv4.dns "192.168.40.3"
```

If the connection that is being modified relates to a traditional `ifcfg-` script, the corresponding file is also edited with the previous `nmcli` command. This is the case with the connection that we have modified. We can view the changes by looking at the file that `nmcli` modified:

```
$ sudo cat /etc/sysconfig/network-scripts/ifcfg-eno16777736
```

To implement changes, we can restart the `NetworkManger` service as follows:

```
$ sudo systemctl restart NetworkManager
```

We can now perform the DNS lookup with dig without the need to specify the address of our server:

```
$ dig www.packtpub.com
```

Here, we have been able to configure the local client to resolve hostnames from the locally configured DNS server.

 As a quick solution, editing the `/etc/resolv.conf` file will work, but it may be overwritten if the changes are not made with the NetworkManager service.

Configuring the DNS zone

One reason to configure a local DNS server is to provide a centralized configuration for name lookups for your local servers. We will now look at how to configure a DNS zone to provide a name resolution for local servers. We will configure a zone called `tup.local.`; using the local suffix will ensure that the zone is configured locally and only available to DNS servers we configure with this zone.

As a caching-only DNS server, we have not hosted DNS zones thus far. A DNS zone is simply a text file that houses hostnames to IP address mappings. We can see? which zones we host in the `/etc/named.conf` file. Zone files are stored in the `/var/named` directory.

Referencing the zone from /etc/named.conf

Within the bind configuration file, we must point to the zone file. The following example illustrates how this can be achieved:

Open `named.conf` using the following command:

```
$ sudo vi /etc/named.conf
```

Add the following section at the end of the file:

```
zone "tup.local." IN {
  type master;
  file "named.tup";
};
```

Do not forget the dot after the domain name: `tup.local.`

With the file configured and saved, we can check the configuration file as before:

```
$ sudo named-checkconf
```

Creating the zone file

We have configured the DNS server to point to the `named.tup` file. By default, this file needs to exist within the `/var/named/` directory on RHEL 7.1. This directory location is dictated by the directory directive in the main options of the `named.conf` file. This extract is taken from the `/etc/named.conf` file and shows the configuration of the directory root:

```
directory       "/var/named";
```

First, create an empty zone file and set the permissions so that it can be read by the DNS server. The `touch` command will create an empty file. We set the permissions to be readable/writable by the user owner and only readable by the group owner. Finally, we set the permissions for the group owner of the file to named (the group used by the DNS server):

```
$ sudo touch /var/named/named.tup
$ sudo chmod 640 /var/named/named.tup
$ sudo chgrp named /var/named/named.tup
```

With the file and permissions in place, we can edit the file as root using `sudo`, so it reads similar to the following screenshot:

```
$ORIGIN tup.local.
$TTL 1D
@           IN  SOA   ns1 root (
                               1        ; serial
                               1D       ; refresh
                               1H       ; retry
                               1W       ; expire
                               3H )     ; minimum
                      NS       ns1
ns1                   A        192.168.40.3
```

We can interpret the preceding screenshot line by line as follows:

- `$ORIGIN tup.local.`: This sets the name of the DNS domain to be appended to all names not ending in a dot.

- `$TTL 1D`: This directive sets the default time that records may be retrieved from cache **TTL (Time To Live)**. The value is normally in seconds, but we can use letters defining larger units, such as H for hours, D for days, or even W for weeks. It's possible to overwrite this default value within an individual DNS record. The larger the value assigned to TTL, the longer it will take to propagate changes on the Internet because records may still be served from cache for the TTL time period. The shorter the TTL is set, shorter the time to propagate changes, but more lookups will be performed on the server.

- `@ IN SOA ns1 root ( ... )`: This sets the **Start Of Authority (SOA)** record for the `tup.local.` DNS domain. The @ symbol represents this domain and the SOA record is set to the `ns1.tup.local` computer. Remember `$ORIGIN` and the e-mail contact is `root@tup.local.`. The brackets contain the serial number and timeouts used in the domain. The expiry record is overwritten by the `$TTL` directive where it's used.

- `NS ns1`: This sets the name server record for the domain. If we have additional slave servers, we can add more NS records in the zone.

- `ns1 A 192.168.40.3`: This sets the IP address mapping for the `ns1.tup.local.` server to the IP address we have set on the system. A single A represents an IPv4 address mapping, while AAAA will represent on IPv6 mapping.

When we complete the edit, we can check the zone syntax and integrity. In the command line, we enter the following command:

```
$ sudo named-checkzone tup.local. /var/named/named.tup
```

The output should be similar to the following screenshot from the demonstration system:

```
[andrew@redhat7 etc]$ sudo named-checkzone tup.local. /var/named/named.tup
zone tup.local/IN: loaded serial 1
OK
[andrew@redhat7 etc]$
```

Having edited the /etc/named.conf file and implemented the new zone /var/named/named.tup database file, we are now ready to restart the service. We have also checked named.conf with the named-checkconf command and the zone file with the named-checkzone command, so we can be reassured of the integrity of the changes we have made; with this in mind, we will restart the service with systemctl:

```
$ sudo systemctl restart named
```

We can use dig or even just ping to check the operation of the zone now:

```
$ ping ns1.tup.local
$ dig ns1.tup.local
```

Although we have only added a single record, there is nothing stopping us from adding more records as required. The serial number is normally incremented after zone changes, but it's used more to indicate when the changes have been made. Slave servers should synchronize these changes. If you have only the master server, there is no need to increment the serial number. Later in this chapter, we will add an **MX** or **Mail Exchange** record to support the use of e-mail delivery in the out domain.

Configuring a DHCP server

The **DHCP (Dynamic Host Configuration Protocol)** server is used to assign IP addresses to network hosts, rather than having to statically assign records to each host. This is, of course, particularly useful where guest devices—such as mobile phones and tablets—connect to you network.

On Red Hat Enterprise Linux 7, a single DHCP server can supply IPv4 and IPv6 configurations. Each configuration has its own separate file: /etc/dhcp/dhcpd.conf for IPv4 configurations and /etc/dhcpd/dhcpd6.conf for IPv6 configurations. Additionally, if you are used to the previous editions of Red Hat, there is no longer any need to configure the interface in /etc/sysconfig/dhcp. RHEL 7 will automatically listen on all interfaces that match a subnet definition in the dhcpd.conf or dhcpd6.conf file. In other words, interfaces that the DHCP server will listen for DHCP requests will match those interfaces that have addresses within the defined DHCP subnet.

If you have not configured the DNS server on the same system, you will need to create an empty lease file before the service will start, as shown in the following command:

```
$ sudo touch /var/lib/dhcpd/dhcpd.leases
```

You can install the DHCP Server using the following command line:

```
$ sudo yum install dhcp
```

In this example, we will configure the server to issue the IPv4 address configuration by editing the /etc/dhcp/dhcpd.conf file. The configuration file will be empty, except for a few comments. A simple configuration that is shown as follows, will match the configuration that we have been using on our demo system:

```
$ sudo vi /etc/dhcp/dhcpd.conf
```

The resulting file should be similar to the following screenshot:

```
[andrew@redhat7 ~]$ sudo cat /etc/dhcp/dhcpd.conf
option domain-name "tup.local";
option domain-name-servers 192.168.40.3;
default-lease-time 86400;
max-lease-time 86400;
ddns-update-style none;
log-facility local7;
subnet 192.168.40.0 netmask 255.255.255.0 {
    range 192.168.40.10 192.168.40.254;
    option routers 192.168.40.2;
}
```

Let's interpret the preceding screenshot line by line as follows:

- `option domain-name "tup.local";`: This configures the domain name to append to the client name.

- `option domain-name-servers 192.168.40.3;`: This sets the DNS server or servers. If more than one server is used, addresses are separated by spaces.

- `default-lease-time 86400;`: This is a value specified in seconds, where we set the DHCP lease time. The value of `86400` is one day. The maximum lease time is similar, but it's used only if a client requests a lease time.

- `ddns-update-style none;`: This disables the dynamic DNS, according to which the DHCP server will create DNS entries for clients that are issued with an IP address.

- `log-facility local7;`: This sets the syslog facility that is used by DHCP. Entries in log files will be shown as coming from the `local7` facility. DHCP does not have its own facility entry.

- Then follows subnet definitions, where we describe the network, subnet mask, address, and options that will be issued for the subnet.

With this, we should now be familiar with the next step. Here, we start and enable the service using system:

```
$ sudo systemctl enable dhcpd
$ sudo systemctl start dhcpd
```

> If you are running on a network where a DHCP server is already present, you will need to ensure that it's stopped before stating your own server. This includes the VMware Player and Virtual Box applications that can issue addresses on their private networks through their own DHCP service. Refer to your virtualization software for more help if required.

If you have additional RHEL 7 clients on a network, they can be forced to renew their DHCP leases with the following command:

```
$ sudo dhclient -r <interface>
```

Here is an example:

```
$ sudo dhclient -r enp12s0
```

The preceding command will renew the DHCP lease on the Ethernet PCI card plugged in to the PCI bus address 12 and slot 0. If a lease or leases have been issued by your server, you can check the leases file. This can be read as a standard user with the following command:

```
$ cat /var/lib/dhcpd/dhcpd.leases
```

The following screenshot shows a lease from the demonstration RHEL 7.1 system and the lease for the host named trusty:

```
lease 192.168.40.10 {
  starts 2 2015/01/27 06:46:25;
  ends 3 2015/01/28 06:46:25;
  cltt 2 2015/01/27 06:46:25;
  binding state active;
  next binding state free;
  rewind binding state free;
  hardware ethernet 00:0c:29:0b:e1:06;
  client-hostname "trusty";
}
```

With the DHCP server in place, we will move on to how to configure our basic networking services with a DNS and DHCP server. We will make this a little better by looking at time services.

Configuring time services on RHEL 7

One of the essential services on your network is the supply of accurate time. This is required for authentication with Active Directory or other Kerberos-based mechanisms and to make timestamps useful in log files.

Network Time Protocol (NTP) uses UDP and the traditional port 123. This protocol dictates the number of seconds that have elapsed since midnight on January 1, 1900. NTP is 32 bit, which means that the maximum time will be reached in 2036; however, as only the difference in timestamps is used rather than the actual time, the date does not present an issue unlike UNIX time ending in 2038, which is a little more serious.

Once the time service is started and synchronized with another time source, the client time can be changed to match the server's time as long as the time is said to be sane. Insane time is said to be a server, offering a time with more than 1000 seconds offset to the client. Using this level of sanity, a client is prevented from synchronizing with a rogue time source.

It's also possible to deploy **Precision Time Protocol (PTP)**. This works with a hardware or software support on your **Network Interface Card (NIC)**. Firstly, we will look at common NTP implementations and then look at PTP.

The provision of NTP on RHEL 7 can be done via the chronyd or ntpd daemon itself. The chronyd daemon is enabled by default; however, this is really designed for desktops and machines that are often disconnected from networks. Synchronization of time with chronyd is much quicker than ntpd and is therefore suitable for machines that are booted frequently or often suspended. The ntpd daemon is still preferred for servers because it supports more authentication options and can broadcast time over the network.

To help maintain accurate time even when the time server may not be available, both chronyd and ntpd can implement a drift file. The drift file is maintained on the client and shows the offset in the frequency of the local hardware clock and the frequency of the remote time source.

NTP is based on a hierarchy of servers. Each server is assigned a stratum number. The possible start values range from 0 to 15. Stratum 16 indicates that time services are not available. A time server with a stratum value of 0 gets its time from a physical time source (such as a GPS clock or an atomic clock). A stratum 1 server retrieves its time from a stratum 0 server, and so on.

Implementing chronyd

As mentioned in the introduction of this section, `chronyd` is enabled by default on the RHEL 7.1 system we are using for this book. We can see the output of the status subcommand for this service with `systemctl` in the following screenshot:

```
[andrew@redhat7 ~]$ sudo systemctl status chronyd
chronyd.service - NTP client/server
   Loaded: loaded (/usr/lib/systemd/system/chronyd.service; enabled)
   Active: active (running) since Mon 2015-01-26 09:11:59 GMT; 24h ago
 Main PID: 883 (chronyd)
   CGroup: /system.slice/chronyd.service
           └─883 /usr/sbin/chronyd -u chrony

Jan 26 09:11:58 redhat7.tup.com systemd[1]: Starting NTP client/server...
Jan 26 09:11:58 redhat7.tup.com chronyd[883]: chronyd version 1.29.1 starting
Jan 26 09:11:58 redhat7.tup.com chronyd[883]: Linux kernel major=3 minor=10 patch=0
Jan 26 09:11:58 redhat7.tup.com chronyd[883]: hz=100 shift_hz=7 freq_scale=1.00000000 nominal_tick=10000 slew_delta_tick=833 max_tick_bias=1000 shift_pll=2
Jan 26 09:11:59 redhat7.tup.com chronyd[883]: Frequency 0.270 +/- 0.725 ppm read from /var/lib/chrony/drift
Jan 26 09:11:59 redhat7.tup.com systemd[1]: Started NTP client/server.
Jan 26 09:12:28 redhat7.tup.com chronyd[883]: Selected source 82.78.227.6
Jan 26 09:12:28 redhat7.tup.com chronyd[883]: System clock wrong by -0.905643 seconds, adjustment started
Jan 26 09:13:34 redhat7.tup.com chronyd[883]: Selected source 83.231.183.4
[andrew@redhat7 ~]$ 
```

As we can see from the preceding output of `sudo systemctl status`, `chronyd` is described as an NTP client/server. This is similar to what we expect from the traditional `ntpd` daemon. If `chronyd` acts as a service as well, then we should listen on port `123`. We can use the `netstat` command to display this. If we use the command with root privileges, we also see that the service holding the port open is `chronyd`. The `-p` option displays this, but requires root privileges.

We run the following command:

`$ sudo netstat -aunp | grep 123`

The output is shown in the following screenshot:

```
[andrew@redhat7 ~]$ sudo netstat -aunp | grep 123
udp        0      0 0.0.0.0:123             0.0.0.0:*                           883/chronyd
udp6       0      0 :::123                  :::*                                883/chronyd
[andrew@redhat7 ~]$ 
```

Going beyond what the output of `systemctl status` can display to use, we can see more detail on the synchronization status of `chronyd` using the `chronyc` command-line tool. Hopefully, you can see the pattern in the names now: `chronyd` for the service or daemon and `chronyc` for the command-line tool.

To show which server has been selected and the status of synchronization, we will use the following command:

```
$ chronyc tracking
```

The following screenshot shows the output of the chronyc command. If you look carefully at the output, you will see the command and then the output that follows the issuance of the same:

```
[andrew@redhat7 ~]$ chronyc tracking
Reference ID    : 83.231.183.4 (dnscache-slough.eu.verio.net)
Stratum         : 3
Ref time (UTC)  : Tue Jan 27 10:17:39 2015
System time     : 0.000367421 seconds slow of NTP time
Last offset     : -0.001594824 seconds
RMS offset      : 0.000622790 seconds
Frequency       : 0.889 ppm fast
Residual freq   : -0.097 ppm
Skew            : 0.233 ppm
Root delay      : 0.026379 seconds
Root dispersion : 0.032379 seconds
Update interval : 2066.6 seconds
Leap status     : Normal
[andrew@redhat7 ~]$
```

Reference ID shows the current server that we use to synchronize time with. Frequency shows as ppm (parts per million). This indicates the rate at which the system clock can become wrong if it was not synchronized. The value here of 0.8 means that after 1,000,000 seconds of not synchronizing, the clock will have an inaccuracy of 0.8 seconds; not at all bad. Update Interval shows how frequently we are currently synchronizing This expands to a much larger value than possible with ntpd being limited to 2 ^ 10 seconds (1024). This interval is quite permissible, given the accuracy of our clock.

With the following command, we can display all servers that we have configured to synchronize with:

```
$ chronyc sources
```

If we want an on screen display of the meaning of columns, we can use the -v option. The output is shown in the following screenshot:

```
[andrew@redhat7 ~]$ chronyc sources -v
210 Number of sources = 4

  .-- Source mode  '^' = server, '=' = peer, '#' = local clock.
 / .- Source state '*' = current synced, '+' = combined , '-' = not combined,
| /   '?' = unreachable, 'x' = time may be in error, '~' = time too variable.
||                                             .- xxxx [ yyyy ] +/- zzzz
||                                            /   xxxx = adjusted offset,
||          Log2(Polling interval) -.        |    yyyy = measured offset,
||                                    \       |    zzzz = estimated error.
||                                     |      |
MS Name/IP address          Stratum Poll Reach LastRx Last sample
===============================================================================
^* dnscache-slough.eu.verio.   2   10   377   842    +26us[ -942us] +/-   43ms
^- alvo.fungus.at              3    6   377    26    +24ms[  +24ms] +/-   95ms
^+ ntp2.adacor.com             2   10   377   583  +1264us[+1264us] +/-  106ms
^+ 82-78-227-6.rdsnet.ro       2   10   377   746   -791us[ -791us] +/-   57ms
[andrew@redhat7 ~]$
```

If we want to synchronize ourselves with one of our own local time servers, we can edit the /etc/chrony.conf configuration file. It will seem reasonable to allocate one server on your network as a time server and use this server as a time reference for the network. The single server then can synchronize with external time sources. This ensures accurate time to all servers on the network while maintaining a small Internet footprint, thus limiting servers that need to access the time servers on the Internet.

The server directive within the configuration file defines potential synchronization partners. To set a bias towards your local server, the prefer option can be used. The following screenshot shows my edited file, where I leave just one of the original entries and add my own local time source:

```
[andrew@redhat7 ~]$ cat /etc/chrony.conf
server 192.168.0.3 iburst prefer
server 1.rhel.pool.ntp.org iburst
stratumweight 0
driftfile /var/lib/chrony/drift
rtcsync
makestep 10 3
bindcmdaddress 127.0.0.1
bindcmdaddress ::1
keyfile /etc/chrony.keys
commandkey 1
generatecommandkey
noclientlog
logchange 0.5
logdir /var/log/chrony
[andrew@redhat7 ~]$
```

For any changes to take effect, the `chronyd` service should be restarted:

```
$ sudo systemctl restart chronyd
```

The frequency of synchronization will start slowly and gradually rise to match the accuracy of the offset frequency. Checking the output of `chronyc` tracking soon after the restart will show a value of 64 seconds for `Update Frequency`; however, this will increase to a larger interval over time.

Implementing ntpd

If you want to revert to the traditional `ntpd` daemon for time services, you can install the `ntp` package. The main advantage of the traditional package is the option of broadcast and stronger **ACL (Access Control List)**. To install the package, you can use the following command:

```
$ sudo yum install ntp
```

The configuration file is located at `/etc/ntp.conf` and is not similar to the `chrony` file. When we edit `ntp.conf` in a similar way to `chrony.conf`, we will be able to configure a local server as before, as shown in the following screenshot:

```
driftfile /var/lib/ntp/drift
restrict default nomodify notrap nopeer noquery
restrict 127.0.0.1
restrict ::1
server 192.168.0.3 iburst prefer
server 1.rhel.pool.ntp.org iburst
includefile /etc/ntp/crypto/pw
keys /etc/ntp/keys
disable monitor
```

The additional ACLs that we find here are defined using the `restrict` keyword. The local host address is not restricted at all, although everyone else is affected by the default restriction.

The default restriction is explained here:

- `nomodify`: This prevents any changes to the configuration via the NTP protocol.
- `notrap` : This prevents `ntpdc` control traps that are designed for use by the remote logging program.

- nopeer :This prevents peer associations from being created, where 50 percent adjustments are made by each peer.

- noquery :This prevents information on the status of the time server being accessed. Do not confuse this with preventing access to a time server. This option will still allow normal NTP time queries from clients. Should you want to restrict access to the time service, use noserve.

When you are comfortable with the changes made to your /etc/ntp.conf file, we will need first to stop and disable the chronyd service and then enable and start the ntpd service:

```
$ sudo systemctl stop chronyd
$ sudo systemctl disable chronyd
$ sudo systemctl enable ntpd
$ sudo systemctl start ntpd
```

To query the status of a service, we will use the ntpq -p command. The output is shown in the following screenshot, indicating on my system that the server being used to synchronize with is 192.168.0.3 (indicated by asterix):

```
[andrew@redhat7 ~]$ ntpq -p
     remote           refid      st t when poll reach   delay   offset  jitter
==============================================================================
*192.168.0.3     193.219.61.110   2 u   26   64    7    0.653    0.455   0.049
 weyoun3.cord.de 192.53.103.104   2 u   24   64    7   34.451    0.822   0.533
[andrew@redhat7 ~]$
```

Implementing PTP on RHEL 7

Precision Time Protocol (PTP) like NTP is used to synchronize clocks on a network, but unlike NTP, if PTP is used with hardware support that can achieve sub-microsecond accuracy; support for PTP comes from your NIC in either software or hardware forms. The linuxptp package provides ptp4l and phc2sys programs (PTP for Linux and physical clock to system clock). However, phc2sys is only needed for hardware timestamping. Although implemented within NICs, many networking components (including switches) support PTP in software or hardware modes, thus enabling servers to synchronize time with their switch. The process is far more automated than traditional NTP and more accurate with each clock running the best master software that can select the best master to synchronize with. It's best suited to Enterprise networks because switches will often provide time to devices they serve.

Many NICs support software timestamping, but to query your own interface, use the following command, which will display the timestamping capabilities of your selected interface:

```
$ ethtool -T eno16777736
```

Adjust the preceding command to match the interface that you wish to interrogate. For the software support, we need to find the following lines in the output:

- SOF_TIMESTAMPING_SOFTWARE
- SOF_TIMESTAMPING_TX_SOFTWARE
- SOF_TIMESTAMPING_RX_SOFTWARE

For the hardware support, we will need the following options:

- SOF_TIMESTAMPING_RAW_HARDWARE
- SOF_TIMESTAMPING_TX_HARDWARE
- SOF_TIMESTAMPING_RX_HARDWARE

The output from my system is shown in the following screenshot:

```
[andrew@redhat7 ~]$ ethtool -T eno16777736
Time stamping parameters for eno16777736:
Capabilities:
        software-transmit      (SOF_TIMESTAMPING_TX_SOFTWARE)
        software-receive       (SOF_TIMESTAMPING_RX_SOFTWARE)
        software-system-clock  (SOF_TIMESTAMPING_SOFTWARE)
PTP Hardware Clock: none
Hardware Transmit Timestamp Modes: none
Hardware Receive Filter Modes: none
[andrew@redhat7 ~]$
```

To install linuxptp on the system, we can use the following command to install from standard Red Hat repositories:

```
$ sudo yum install linuxptp
```

The services can be run from the command line as a simple test. However, prior to this, we should stop NTP if it's running. This is shown in the following commands:

```
$ sudo systemctl disable ntpd
$ sudo systemctl stop ntpd
```

To start a service from the command line rather than as a daemon, we can verify that it works using the following command:

```
$ sudo ptp4l -i eno16777736 -m -S
```

This starts the service using the interface we specify using the -i option, we ask output to go to the screen with the -m option and we set the software mode with the -S option.

The service will listen on UDP ports 319 and 320. The output of the command is shown in the following screenshot:

```
[andrew@redhat7 ~]$ sudo ptp4l -i eno16777736 -m -S
[sudo] password for andrew:
ptp4l[106085.688]: port 1: INITIALIZING to LISTENING on INITIALIZE
ptp4l[106085.689]: port 0: INITIALIZING to LISTENING on INITIALIZE
ptp4l[106092.238]: port 1: LISTENING to MASTER on ANNOUNCE_RECEIPT_TIMEOUT_EXPIRES
ptp4l[106092.238]: selected best master clock 000c29.fffe.57efc4
ptp4l[106092.238]: assuming the grand master role
```

Once we are happy with our configuration, we can create the startup configuration file and adjust the sysconfig file. We will start with the sysconfig file:

```
$ sudo vi /etc/sysconfig/ptp4l
```

Remove the interface option at the end of the line. The file should read the same as the following screenshot:

```
[andrew@redhat7 ~]$
[andrew@redhat7 ~]$ cat /etc/sysconfig/ptp4l
OPTIONS="-f /etc/ptp4l.conf"
[andrew@redhat7 ~]$
```

Next, we will rename the existing configuration and create a minimal configuration that supports the same options that we used from the command line as follows:

```
$ sudo mv /etc/ptp4l.conf /etc/ptp4l.conf.orig
$ sudo vi /etc/ptp4l.conf
```

The `ptp4l.conf` file should be similar to adjusting the interface in order to match the interface on your own system. The following screenshot shows the `ptp4l.conf` file on my system:

```
[andrew@redhat7 ~]$ cat /etc/ptp4l.conf
[global]
verbose 1
time_stamping software
[eno16777736]
[andrew@redhat7 ~]$
```

We are now ready to implement `ptp4l` as a service. With the `systemctl` command, we will be able to enable and start the service, as shown in the following commands:

```
$ sudo systemctl enable ptp4l
$ sudo systemctl start ptp4l
```

Using the `status` subcommand to `systemctl` as in the previous commands, we will see the output similar to the following, indicating that the service has started and looking for clock announcements:

```
[andrew@redhat7 ~]$ sudo systemctl status ptp4l
[sudo] password for andrew:
ptp4l.service - Precision Time Protocol (PTP) service
   Loaded: loaded (/usr/lib/systemd/system/ptp4l.service; disabled)
   Active: active (running) since Tue 2015-01-27 14:48:00 GMT; 9min ago
 Main PID: 42197 (ptp4l)
   CGroup: /system.slice/ptp4l.service
           └─42197 /usr/sbin/ptp4l -f /etc/ptp4l.conf

Jan 27 14:48:00 redhat7.tup.com ptp4l[42197]: ptp4l[106577.048]: port 1: INITIALIZING to LISTENING on INITIALIZE
Jan 27 14:48:00 redhat7.tup.com ptp4l[42197]: ptp4l[106577.049]: port 0: INITIALIZING to LISTENING on INITIALIZE
Jan 27 14:48:00 redhat7.tup.com ptp4l[42197]: [106577.048] port 1: INITIALIZING to LISTENING on INITIALIZE
Jan 27 14:48:00 redhat7.tup.com ptp4l[42197]: [106577.049] port 0: INITIALIZING to LISTENING on INITIALIZE
Jan 27 14:48:07 redhat7.tup.com ptp4l[42197]: ptp4l[106584.093]: port 1: LISTENING to MASTER on ANNOUNCE_RECEIPT_TIMEOUT_EXPIRES
Jan 27 14:48:07 redhat7.tup.com ptp4l[42197]: ptp4l[106584.093]: selected best master clock 000c29.fffe.57efc4
Jan 27 14:48:07 redhat7.tup.com ptp4l[42197]: ptp4l[106584.093]: assuming the grand master role
Jan 27 14:48:07 redhat7.tup.com ptp4l[42197]: [106584.093] port 1: LISTENING to MASTER on ANNOUNCE_RECEIPT_TIMEOUT_EXPIRES
Jan 27 14:48:07 redhat7.tup.com ptp4l[42197]: [106584.093] selected best master clock 000c29.fffe.57efc4
Jan 27 14:48:07 redhat7.tup.com ptp4l[42197]: [106584.093] assuming the grand master role
[andrew@redhat7 ~]$ sudo systemctl status ptp4l
[sudo] password for andrew:
ptp4l.service - Precision Time Protocol (PTP) service
   Loaded: loaded (/usr/lib/systemd/system/ptp4l.service; disabled)
   Active: active (running) since Tue 2015-01-27 14:48:00 GMT; 17min ago
 Main PID: 42197 (ptp4l)
   CGroup: /system.slice/ptp4l.service
           └─42197 /usr/sbin/ptp4l -f /etc/ptp4l.conf
```

When the server is running, it may listen for other clock announcements and then negotiate as to which will be the grand master. In the following screenshot taken from the demonstration system, we can view the output of the `systemctl status` command. From the log extract, we can see the election of the new grand master:

```
Jan 27 15:04:49 redhat7.tup.com ptp4l[42197]: ptp4l[107585.597]: port 1: new foreign master 000c29.fffe.b76ccc-1
Jan 27 15:04:49 redhat7.tup.com ptp4l[42197]: [107585.597] port 1: new foreign master 000c29.fffe.b76ccc-1
Jan 27 15:04:53 redhat7.tup.com ptp4l[42197]: ptp4l[107589.598]: selected best master clock 000c29.fffe.b76ccc
Jan 27 15:04:53 redhat7.tup.com ptp4l[42197]: ptp4l[107589.598]: assuming the grand master role
Jan 27 15:04:53 redhat7.tup.com ptp4l[42197]: [107589.598] selected best master clock 000c29.fffe.b76ccc
Jan 27 15:04:53 redhat7.tup.com ptp4l[42197]: [107589.598] assuming the grand master role
```

We have now seen how to implement time services on Linux using either NTP, Cronyd, or PTP. With accurate time, we can now move forward to e-mail and **SMTP (Simple Mail Transfer Protocol)**.

Implementing e-mail delivery on RHEL 7

The default SMTP server used in the current release of RHEL is Postfix; the original Sendmail package is still available, but is no longer the default.

It's normal for the e-mail server to listen on the localhost or loopback address only when using default settings. In this way, local e-mail delivery is possible out of the box. This is used by many services, including the `crond` job schedule manager. If we wanted to enable Postfix to listen on all interfaces and receive messages from remote systems, there is a little configuration required.

Firstly, we will back up and tidy the main configuration file. There is a tendency for many software packages to over comment their configurations. This can cause issues where you think that you have implemented a change; however, it was also set later on and you may not have noticed it. There are 679 lines in the default configuration file: `/etc/postfix/main.cf`. We will back up the file so that we do not lose comments and documentations, but we will also have a new working file with less than 10 percent of the number of lines. The following command shows how this is done:

```
$ sudo sed -i.bak '/^#/d;/^$/d' /etc/postfix/main.cf
```

This reduces the file from 679 lines to 25 lines and is far easier to work with. We can now edit this file without any distractions. We will add two new lines and edit two existing lines to the `/etc/postfix/main.cf` file. This will need to be edited as root.

We will edit the `inet_interfaces = localhost` line so that it reads as follows:

```
inet_interfaces = all
```

This will enable the SMTP service to listen on all interfaces, rather than just the loopback addresses.

We also need to make sure that we receive e-mails for the correct host and domain. This is controlled through the `mydestination` directive; however, we have to add the `myhostname` and `mydomain` directives before the `mydestination` line. These are the two lines that we add. We also need to add `$mydomain` to the existing `mydestination` line. On my system, these lines are set as follows:

```
myhostname = ns1.tup.local
mydomain = tup.local
mydestination = $myhostname, localhost.$mydomain, localhost, $mydomain
```

The following screenshot shows the top few lines of the file where these changes have been implemented:

```
queue_directory = /var/spool/postfix
command_directory = /usr/sbin
daemon_directory = /usr/libexec/postfix
data_directory = /var/lib/postfix
mail_owner = postfix
inet_interfaces = all
inet_protocols = all
myhostname = ns1.tup.local
mydomain = tup.local
mydestination = $myhostname, localhost.$mydomain, localhost, $mydomain
```

With these edits is place, we can save the file and restart the SMTP service. The following command shows how to restart the Postfix SMTP service:

```
$ sudo systemctl restart postfix
```

Adding an MX record to the DNS server

If we are to receive an e-mail for the domain, we will need an MX record (e-mail exchange) to the DNS database that we created earlier in this section. The file that was used earlier for the `tup.local`. DNS domain was `/var/named/named.tup`. The record that we add for the MX or Mail Exchange record should be similar to the following line:

```
tup.local.  MX  10  ns1
```

With this setting, we configure the MX or Mail Exchange priority to 10. The lowest priority MX Record is the e-mail server that is used first if more than one e-mail server record exists.

The updated zone file is shown in the following screenshot:

```
$ORIGIN tup.local.
$TTL 1D
@          IN SOA  ns1 root (
                              1        ; serial
                              1D       ; refresh
                              1H       ; retry
                              1W       ; expire
                              3H )     ; minimum
                   NS         ns1
ns1                A          192.168.40.3
tup.local.         MX 10      ns1
```

With these updates in place, we can check the zone and restart the server. For convenience, the commands are listed here:

```
$ sudo named-checkzone tup.local /var/named/named.tup
```

```
$ sudo systemctl restart named
```

We can verify that DNS is working with the following command:

```
$ dig -t MX tup.local
```

To test the e-mail delivery, we should be able to send e-mails to the domain:

```
$ mail root@tup.local
```

We will be prompted for the Subject message and then we can enter the e-mail we wish. To end an e-mail, we will include a line with just the period or a dot character and nothing else. This should be delivered to the root on your system being recognized as the e-mail server for the domain.

To view the message system working in more detail, we can take a look at the log files. To see the recent activity, we can use the tail command as follows:

```
$ sudo tail /var/log/maillog
```

We now have a simple e-mail server to go with time, DNS, and DHCP services.

Summary

In this chapter, you learned how to configure some of the fundamental network services often associated with Linux. We started off with how to set up the name resolution using DNS and ended up finishing on the same topic as we added e-mail server records to DNS. Having looked at DNS, we stayed alliteratively with D and studied DHCP, thus allowing a supply of IP configuration to the network. This took us to the complexities of the different time services that are on offer with `chronyd`, `ntpd`, and `ptp41`. At the end of the chapter, we looked at a simple configuration of the Postfix SMTP server on RHEL 7. This should give you a simple overview of services that you can expect to work with on a day-to-day basis with Enterprise Linux.

In the next chapter, we will see what is new on RHEL 7 and 7.1 and how to set up iSCSI storage services. You will find that the ISCSI target is now kernel-based and works very differently to the previous iSCSI target service on RHEL 6.

4

Implementing iSCSI SANs

A really big change that you may notice on RHEL 7 compared with earlier releases is that the iSCSI target service is now part of the kernel. This is part and parcel of the move to version 3.x.x of the Linux kernel that we see in the latest Enterprise offering from Raleigh, NC. The management and configuration of the iSCSI server or target is completely revamped. You will soon learn how to share disks and partitions with devices on your network. In doing so, we will look at how to configure the following prerequisites:

- The iSCSI target (server)
- Logical volumes with LVM
- Installing the `targetd` service and `targetcli` tools
- Managing iSCSI targets using `targetcli`
- The iSCSI initiator client

The iSCSI target (server)

The iSCSI target is a software that makes disk space available on a network. This service shares disks rather than filesystems and establishes a **Storage Area Network (SAN)**. This SAN storage can be used so that servers can share same disks, a situation that is often required where other network services are clustered and need access to shared disks on the network. It's usual that only one server will have access to each shared disk at any one time. The iSCSI target can share complete disks, but it's often more efficient to share the exact space required by the client through logical volumes implemented with LVMs. As well as sharing block devices, it's also possible to create files and share the file space as disks through the target server.

The disk IO passes through standard network connections to iSCSI servers. So, the faster the network connection, the better the storage performance. Although iSCSI will work on 1 GB Ethernet networks, 10 GB Ethernet is preferred for Enterprise usage. Having said that, for home or small office use, you will find that 1 GB network speed should be fine (especially if you can define a separate network segment to isolate the iSCSI traffic from the rest of your network). The default TCP port used by the target is 3260.

Managing logical volumes with LVM

Although we can share the entire disk space or disk partitions, it really makes sense to share just the disk space that a client service requires. So, for example, if a web server requires 20 GB of space for web files, we can share just that absolute space, rather than the whole disk that may be terabytes in size. To do so, we will create logical volumes and share these as block devices. To implement LVMs, we create three objects:

- **Physical volumes**: This represents the raw disk space as disk partitions. When we use partitions, the partition type should be set to Linux LVM with an ID of 8E using the fdisk partitioning tool.

- **Volume groups**: This aggregates physical volumes together so that the disk space can be consumed to logical volumes.

- **Logical volumes**: This represents the block device that can be shared. It consumes space that is allocated from volume groups.

On the demonstration RHEL 7.1 system that we will use for this course, I have three disks attached currently. We can use part of the space on the third drive for the LVM system. We will start by partitioning the third disk (currently unpartitioned) so that we can use some elements of this disk for LVM and other elements for other filesystems.

Partitioning the disk

Using the fdisk command, we can partition the disk as required. We will use a single extended partition and create logical partitions therein. This is purely to allow many partitions that we can use here and in later chapters:

```
$ sudo fdisk /dev/sdc
```

Take care with the device name that you use!

When you run the `fdisk` command, you will be presented with a menu. The `m` command can be used to see menu choices, but we can use `n` to create a new partition and then `e` to create an extended partition. We will enter to accept the defaults for the partition number and the start and end sectors. We will set the extended partition to use the complete disk.

Now, we will use `n` again to create another new partition; this time we will choose `l` for logical reasons. The partition number will default to `5`, so `/dev/sdc5` in my case3. We can accept the default starting sector, but we will limit the size to 200 M with `+200M` as the ending sector. The following screenshot illustrates this setting:

```
Command (m for help): n
Partition type:
   p   primary (0 primary, 1 extended, 3 free)
   l   logical (numbered from 5)
Select (default p): l
Adding logical partition 5
First sector (4096-4194303, default 4096):
Using default value 4096
Last sector, +sectors or +size{K,M,G} (4096-4194303, default 4194303): +200M
```

With the settings entered and still within the interactive `fdisk` command, we can use the `t` option to set a type. By default, this will be set to `83`. When you enter `t`, you will be asked for the partition number, which will default to `5`. To type the partition code, we will use `8e` for LVM. Subsequently, we will use `p` to print the configuration and then `w` to save the changes and exit the program.

Creating the physical volume

So far, we have created a partition for LVM to use, but this is not part of any LVM system yet. To mark it as available, we will use the `pvcreate` command:

```
$ sudo pvcreate /dev/sdc5
```

To display the LVM physical volume on a system, you can use either the `pvs` command or the `pvscan` command as the root user. The output of `sudo pvscan` is shown in the following screenshot:

```
[andrew@redhat7 ~]$ sudo pvscan
  PV /dev/sda2   VG rhel   lvm2 [9.51 GiB / 40.00 MiB free]
  PV /dev/sdc5             lvm2 [200.00 MiB]
  Total: 2 [9.70 GiB] / in use: 1 [9.51 GiB] / in no VG: 1 [200.00 MiB]
```

The output shows that we already have LVM in use on this system because this is the default on RHEL and many other systems. The new PV is shown as /dev/sdc5, but without any membership of a **volume group (VG)**.

Creating the volume group

As we already have a volume group in place, we will use that group and extend it to include the new PV using the vgextend command. We want to keep this volume group separate and solely for space to be shared with the iSCSI Target. For this reason, we will create a new volume group with the vgcreate command, as shown in the following code example:

```
$ sudo vgcreate iscsi /dev/sdc5
```

Using this command, we will create a new volume group called iscsi and use /dev/sdc5 PV.

Similar to physical volumes, we can use vgscan or vgs to display information on the volume groups that are available. The output from sudo vgs is shown in the following screenshot:

```
[andrew@redhat7 ~]$ sudo vgs
  VG    #PV #LV #SN Attr   VSize   VFree
  iscsi   1   0   0 wz--n- 196.00m 196.00m
  rhel    1   2   0 wz--n-   9.51g  40.00m
```

From the preceding output, we can see that our newly created VG named iscsi has a single PV connected to it, but as yet, no logical volumes (LV), which we will create next.

Creating logical volumes

Logical volumes (LVs) are block device units that we can use locally or (in our case) share via iSCSI. We create LVs using the lvcreate command. An example is as follows:

```
$ sudo lvcreate -n web -L 100M iscsi
```

As is normal, we will not use all of the available space and just use the space requested by the web team for their new web volume. The -L option sets the size we allocate. We will allocate 100M; -n sets the name to web in this case, whereas the VG name is appended to the end of the command string.

This command will create a block device in the /dev directory, but this device is usually accessed via symbolic links. The following two symbolic links will be created:

- /dev/mapper/iscsi-web
- /dev/iscsi/web

In our case, these link to the /dev/dm-2 block device. On your system, the actual block device name will depend on how many existing LVs you have. This is why the OS uses symbolic links because this name is determinable, whereas the actual block device name is not so determinable.

If you can detect a pattern here, you will realize that, in order to display information about LVs on a system, we can use lvs or lvscan. The output of the sudo lvscan command is shown in the following screenshot:

```
[andrew@redhat7 ~]$ sudo lvscan
  ACTIVE            '/dev/rhel/swap' [1.00 GiB] inherit
  ACTIVE            '/dev/rhel/root' [8.47 GiB] inherit
  ACTIVE            '/dev/iscsi/web' [100.00 MiB] inherit
```

At this stage, we have a working block device that we can use with the iSCSI target service to share between servers on the network. We will now look at how to configure the iSCSI target on RHEL 7.1.

Installing the targetd service and targetcli tools

To manage the kernel-based iSCSI Target service on RHEL 7, we will need to install the targetd and targetcli package, as shown in the following command:

```
$ sudo yum install targetd targetcli
```

From the output, we can see that additional packages are installed; however, it's more interesting to see how Python is used as a major tool to manage iSCSI. The following screenshot is an extract from the command line output:

```
=================================================================================
 Package                                      Arch
=================================================================================
Installing:
 targetcli                                    noarch
 targetd                                      noarch
Installing for dependencies:
 PyYAML                                       x86_64
 libyaml                                      x86_64
 lvm2-python-libs                             x86_64
 pyparsing                                    noarch
 python-configshell                           noarch
 python-kmod                                  x86_64
 python-rtslib                                noarch
 python-setproctitle                          x86_64
 python-urwid                                 x86_64

Transaction Summary
=================================================================================
Install  2 Packages (+9 Dependent packages)
```

Although the iSCSI target runs as part of the kernel, the targetd package provides a service. This service is used to load the iSCSI target configuration. This is all that targetd does, so we never need to start this service as such; just ensure that targetd is enabled for autostart, as shown in the following command:

```
$ sudo systemctl enable targetd
```

> Once the system startup enables the targetd service, it ensures that the targetcli restoreconfig command is executed. It also ensures that the current configuration is loaded on boot.

We have now installed management tools for the targetcli iSCSI target and the targetd service, which provides a mechanism to enable the configuration to be read at boot time. We will now move on to how to configure the target with targetcli.

Managing iSCSI targets with targetcli

The targetcli command is a shell to view, edit, save, and load the iSCSI target configuration. When you look at the configuration, you will see that targetcli provides a hierarchical structure in a similar way to a filesystem.

To invoke the `targetcli` shell, we will run this command as root using `sudo`. You will see that on the first run of the command, a preferences file is created. This is illustrated in the following screenshot:

```
[andrew@redhat7 ~]$ sudo targetcli
[sudo] password for andrew:
Warning: Could not load preferences file /root/.targetcli/prefs.bin.
targetcli shell version 2.1.fb37
Copyright 2011-2013 by Datera, Inc and others.
For help on commands, type 'help'.

/>
```

As you can see in the preceding output, you can enter `help` to display a list of commands that can be entered. To view the available configuration objects, we can use the `ls` command. The output is shown in the following screenshot:

```
/> ls
o- / ............................................. [...]
  o- backstores .................................. [...]
  | o- block .................... [Storage Objects: 0]
  | o- fileio ................... [Storage Objects: 0]
  | o- pscsi .................... [Storage Objects: 0]
  | o- ramdisk .................. [Storage Objects: 0]
  o- iscsi .............................. [Targets: 0]
  o- loopback ........................... [Targets: 0]
/>
```

We will work with `backstores` objects to start with so that we can add it to the LVM block device in the configuration in addition to the `fileio` backstore. As the name suggests, this will be a file within the filesystem; we can share this to a network as a virtual disk.

Creating storage backstores

We will work from the root of the `targetcli` configuration; this should be exactly where we are, but we can always use the `pwd` command to display our working directory. If required, we can change it to the root of the configuration with `cd /`.

While using the `targetcli` command, we can use *CTRL + L* to clear the screen as we would in Bash, but most importantly, the *Tab* key completion works, so we do not need to type the complete name or path to objects and properties.

To create a new `block`, back store on the LVM LV that we created earlier in this section. If we recall, this was `/dev/iscsi/web`:

`/> backstore/block/ create web_lv /dev/iscsi/web`

This will create the block backstore with a name called `web_lv`. Using the `ls` command again will list the additional object within the hierarchy. In the following screenshot, we see the creation of the backstore and the subsequent listing:

```
/> backstores/block create web_lv /dev/iscsi/web
Created block storage object web_lv using /dev/iscsi/web.
/> ls
o- / ............................................................................ [...]
  o- backstores ................................................................. [...]
  | o- block .................................................... [Storage Objects: 1]
  | | o- web_lv .................................... [/dev/iscsi/web (100.0MiB) write-thru deactivated]
  | o- fileio ................................................... [Storage Objects: 0]
  | o- pscsi .................................................... [Storage Objects: 0]
  | o- ramdisk ................................................. [Storage Objects: 0]
  o- iscsi ........................................................... [Targets: 0]
  o- loopback ........................................................ [Targets: 0]
/>
```

We will also add a new backstore called `fileio`. The creation of the new backstore is similar to the root of the configuration:

`/> backstores/fileio create file_store /tmp/fs 100M`

This command will create the backstore and the physical file, which we will use as a virtual disk. If the file already exists, we omit the size parameter. Both these objects will show in the listing if we choose to use the `ls` command again.

Other backstore types include `pscsi` and `ramdisk`. These represent `Passthrough SCSI` connections that refer to physical iSCSI devices and `Memory Based Disks`, which, as with `fileio`, can be created on the fly using `targetcli`.

Creating iSCSI targets

The iSCSI objects that we see in the main list represents iSCSI targets and their properties. Firstly, we will create a simple iSCSI target with default names. We can then delete this object and see how to create our own target with the correct naming convention:

```
/> iscsi/ create
```

This will create an iSCSI target and listen on the TCP port 3260. There will not be any LUNS or backstores connected, and the **IQN (iSCSI Qualified Name)** will be system generated. We can always add the backstore, but most likely, we want to use our own name. So, in this case, we will delete the object. The IQN on my system was generated as iqn.2003-01.org.linux-iscsi.redhat7.x8664:sn.celebea336a2, but do not forget that we can use the *Tab* key completion. So, we do not need to write the complete name while deleting or editing it. The following command displays this, but it may wrap when displayed or printed so that it is executed as a single line of code:

```
/> iscsi/ delete iqn.2003-01.org.linux-iscsi.redhat7.x8664:sn.
celebea336a2
```

We will now create an iSCSI target by supplying a custom IQN. To perform this, we create the object as before, but this time, specify the name that is usually written to contain the date and the reversed DNS name. The following command is an example that we will use in this book:

```
/> iscsi/ create iqn.2015-01.com.tup.rhel7:web
```

IQN starts with iqn, which is followed by the year and month it was created and the reverse DNS name. We can add the description of the target with the :web at the end, indicating that this is a target for the web server.

We can filter what is displayed using the ls command by adding the object hierarchy that we want to list. For example, to list targets, we will use the ls iscsi command.

The output of this command is shown in the following screenshot:

```
/> ls iscsi/
o- iscsi ............................................... [Targets: 1]
  o- iqn.2015-01.com.tup.rhel:web ........................ [TPGs: 1]
    o- tpg1 ...................................... [no-gen-acls, no-auth]
     .o- acls .......................................... [ACLs: 0]
      o- luns .......................................... [LUNs: 0]
      o- portals ..................................... [Portals: 1]
        o- 0.0.0.0:3260 ...................................... [OK]
/>
```

Now we have our customized name for the target, but we still have to add the LUNS or logical units to make the **SAN (Storage Area Network)** effective.

Adding LUNS to the iSCSI target

Staying with the targetcli shell, we will now move on to our target and **TPG (Target Portal Group)** object. Similar to the filesystem, this is achieved using the cd command, as shown in the following command:

```
/> cd iscsi/iqn.2015-01.com.tup.rhel:web/tpg1/
```

We can run ls from here, but the content was included in the previous listing that we ran from the root of the configuration. We have one portal that listens on all IPv4 interfaces on the TCP port 3260. Currently, we have no acls or luns. To add a LUN, we will use the following command, which will utilize the LVM block backstore:

```
/iscsi/iqn.20...rhel:web/tpg1> luns/ create /backstores/block/web_lv
```

This will have an additional side effect of activating a backstore. This can be seen by listing the /backstores object. The command and output are shown in the following screenshot:

```
/iscsi/iqn.20...rhel:web/tpg1> ls /backstores/
o- backstores ......................................................... [...]
  o- block ....................................... [Storage Objects: 1]
  | o- web_lv .................... [/dev/iscsi/web (100.0MiB) write-thru activated]
  o- fileio ...................................... [Storage Objects: 1]
  | o- file_store ............... [/tmp/fs (100.0MiB) write-back deactivated]
  o- pscsi ....................................... [Storage Objects: 0]
  o- ramdisk ..................................... [Storage Objects: 0]
/iscsi/iqn.20...rhel:web/tpg1>
```

Adding ACLS

We are not required to add ACLS, but often we only want a single host, perhaps a virtual cluster device in order to access the LUN. If there is no ACL, we will need to set a property so that the LUN does not default to read only.

To create an ACL, we limit the access from LUN to a given initiator name or names that we mention in **Access Control List (ACL)**. The initiator is the iSCSI client and will have a unique client IQN configured on the initiator in the /etc/iscsi/ initiatorname.iscsi file. If this file is not present, you will need to install the iscsi-initiator-utils package. The filename used to configure the initiator name will be consistent for Linux clients, but will differ for other operating systems. To add an ACL, we will remain with the current configuration hierarchy: /iscsi/iqn... .:web/tpg1 and issue the following command, again written as a single line:

```
/iscsi/iqn.20...rhel:web/tpg1> acls/ create iqn.2015-01.com.tup.web:web
```

This ACL restricts access to the initiator listed within the ACL. Be careful if you ever change the initiator name because the ACL will also need to be updated. The initiator is the iSCSI client.

Using the ls command from this location in the configuration hierarchy, we see the output similar to the following screenshot, which also includes the command to create the ACL:

```
/iscsi/iqn.20...rhel:web/tpg1> acls/ create iqn.2015-01.com.tup.web:web
Created Node ACL for iqn.2015-01.com.tup.web:web
Created mapped LUN 0.
/iscsi/iqn.20...rhel:web/tpg1> ls
o- tpg1 ................................................. [no-gen-acls, no-auth]
  o- acls ................................................................ [ACLs: 1]
  | o- iqn.2015-01.com.tup.web:web ............................... [Mapped LUNs: 1]
  |   o- mapped_lun0 ..................................... [lun0 block/web_lv (rw)]
  o- luns ................................................................ [LUNs: 1]
  | o- lun0 ...................................... [block/web_lv (/dev/iscsi/web)]
  o- portals ........................................................... [Portals: 1]
    o- 0.0.0.0:3260 .......................................................... [OK]
```

If you do not add an ACL, the LUN will be read only. If you require the LUN to be writable, you will need to use the following command in order to set the required attribute:

```
/iscsi/iqn.20...rhel:web/tpg1> set attribute demo_mode_write_protect=0
```

The iSCSI target is now configured. Exiting targetcli should save this configuration, but you may feel safer to manually save your changes.

To do this, return to the root of the configuration and enter the `saveconfig` command, as shown in the following example:

```
/iscsi/iqn.20...rhel:web/tpg1> cd /
/> saveconfig
/> exit
```

 The `targetd` service that we enabled earlier in this chapter runs the `restoreconfig` command from `targetcli`. This is used to load the configuration when the system boots.

With the configuration saved, we can migrate to the client in order to look at the iSCSI Initiator and see the disk sharing at work on our SAN.

Working with the iSCSI Initiator

The iSCSI Initiator or client on RHEL 7 is installed with the `iscsi-initiator-utils` package; you can verify that this is installed on your system using the `yum` command, as shown in the following example:

```
$ yum list iscsi-initiator-utils
```

If it's listed as `Installed`, all well and good, but if it's listed as `Available`, you will need to install it.

For the purpose of this exercise, we will use a separate RHEL 7 system as our initiator and connect it to the existing target. We will need to edit the `/etc/iscsi/initiatorname.iscsi` file on the new RHEL 7 system to ensure that the name is set to match the name we added to the ACL in the earlier section of this chapter; we can display this using the `cat` command, as shown in the following screenshot:

```
[andrewmallett@targetcli Desktop]$ sudo cat /etc/iscsi/initiatorname.iscsi
[sudo] password for andrewmallett:
InitiatorName=iqn.2015-01.com.tup.web:web
[andrewmallett@targetcli Desktop]$ 
```

We will use the main client tool: `iscsiadm`. This was installed with the previously mentioned package. To discover iSCSI LUNS on the target, we will use the following command:

```
$ sudo iscsiadm --mode discovery --type sendtargets \
--portal 192.168.40.3 --discover
```

The output should be similar to the following line:

```
192.168.40.3:3260,1 iqn.2015-01.com.tup.rhel7:web
```

Now, we have seen that we can connect to the iSCSI target and have it sent us the configured LUNS. We should now connect to this LUN and use the same command with the following options:

```
sudo iscsiadm --mode node \
--targetname iqn.2015-01.com.tup.rhel7:web \
--portal 192.168.40.3 --login
```

The following screenshot shows the command and output:

```
[andrewmallett@targetcli ~]$ sudo iscsiadm --mode node --targetname iqn.2015-01.com.tup.rhel:web --portal 192.16
8.40.3 --login
Logging in to [iface: default, target: iqn.2015-01.com.tup.rhel:web, portal: 192.168.40.3,3260] (multiple)
Login to [iface: default, target: iqn.2015-01.com.tup.rhel:web, portal: 192.168.40.3,3260] successful.
```

To the initiator, the shared LUN is now a disk. We can partition and format this disk in a normal manner. We will use `lsblk` to list the various connected block devices. On this system, we can see that it connects as `/dev/sdc` and matches the `100M` size that we assigned, as shown in the following screenshot:

```
sdc                8:32  0  100M  0 disk
```

Using the traditional `fdisk` or `parted` commands, we can create a partition and then format it to be used locally on this system. As we used `fdisk` previously in the chapter to create the partition for LVM interactively, we will see how to manage this from the command line directly with `parted`.

The command will need a disk label in order to create the partition table. This can be set to `msdos` or `gpt`. The `fdisk` command creates the `msdos` label automatically, but this is because it can only work with traditional `msdos` partition tables. Parted can work with `msdos` and `gpt` (GUID partition tables). The `parted` command also allows partitions to be created either interactively or directly from the command line and hence, is scriptable. There is an added complication here, that is, the sectors to start a new partition are not shown. So, we need to figure out the optimal starting sector.

Once you know this for a disk of a given type, this will be the same for similar disks.

To establish the starting sector on a disk, we will read the values from two files: /sys/block/sdc/queue/optimal_io_size and divide this by /sys/block/sdc/queue/physical_block_size.

On the demonstration system, this relates to *4194304 / 512 = 8192*; values from files can be read with the `cat` command as a standard user. Once we are aware of the optimal alignment details, we can label the disk and create the partition with the following commands:

```
$ sudo parted /dev/sdc mklabel msdos
$ sudo parted /dev/sdc mkpart primary 8192s 100%
```

We create a single partition: `/dev/sdc1`. When we start with the optimal starting sector, this partition uses 100 percent of the used disk space.

With this in place, we can format the partition with the filesystem of our choice and mount it in a normal manner. The `iscsid` background service is enabled, but it only runs when required. On reboot, the connection will be remade to the remote iSCSI Storage server so that the `/dev/sdc1` partition will persist on the client. This will happen as long as the default setting is not changed on the initiator. You should check the `/etc/iscsi/iscsid.conf` file and ensure that the setting is done as follows:

```
node.startup = automatic
```

With this in place, which is the default on RHEL 7, the `iscsid` service will reconnect on startup.

Summary

In this chapter, we have seen how ready RHEL 7 is for the Enterprise network to act as a SAN server using the new kernel-based iSCSI target server. The management of the server is now made through Python-based tools, such as `targetcli`, and the `targetd` service is there to load the configuration at boot. We often provide disk storage on demand from logical volumes. We also looked at how to use three components of LVM to make this happen: physical volumes, volume groups, and logical volumes.

With our storage created and shared, we looked at the second RHEL 7 system and how to connect it as an iSCSI Initiator to utilize this shared storage on the iSCSI target. This was managed initially using `iscsiadm`, but the connections are persisted through the `iscsid` service.

In the next chapter, we will take a look at the **BTRFS (Better File System)**, which makes its first appearance on RHEL with version 7. I am sure that you will be impressed with what is on offer with this filesystem.

5
Implementing btrfs

In this chapter, we will investigate what is on offer with btrfs (pronounced as *Better FS*). Although not directly related to networking, we will soon look at how to share filesystems; for this reason and as btrfs is so incredibly good, we will take a look at it right here and right now. Btrfs is a local filesystem that provides the benefits of integrated volume management operations with easy growth and a fault-tolerance built-in the filesystem. It's not fully supported by Red Hat and ships as a technology preview; it has to be said that Red Hat is cautious on this matter because SUSE has had btrfs as their default filesystem since Enterprise Linux 11 SP2 and continues on SLES 12.

In this chapter, we will cover the following topics:

- Overview of btrfs
- Overview of the lab environment
- Creating the btrfs filesystem
- The copy-on-write technology
- Resizing the btrfs filesystem
- Adding devices to the btrfs filesystem
- Mounting multidisk btrfs volumes from /etc/fstab
- Implementing RAID with btrfs
- Optimizing solid state drives
- Point-in-time data backups using snapshots
- Snapshot management with snappers

Overview of btrfs

If there is one thing that Linux is able to offer you at present, it's a choice of filesystems with over 55 kernel-based filesystems on the Linux kernel tree. So, why do we need more? We are already seeing that older filesystems such as xfs are making a second coming with Red Hat championing this original filesystem from SGI. The btrfs filesystem provides a unique solution that combines the management of volume and a filesystem to a unified solution. Btrfs is licensed under the **General Public License (GPL)** and ships as standard on Red Hat Enterprise 7 and 7.1. It does not just provide access to file management, but also provides access to volume and the **Redundant Array of Inexpensive Disks (RAID)** management. This simple administration means that you can create RAID devices or extend volumes using single commands, rather than relying on LVM for logical volumes or mdadm for RAID. Scalability is also a major factor in choosing btrfs. This scales to 16 EB (Exabytes) and brings the following reliability features not found previously:

- Very fast filesystem creation
- Data and metadata checksums
- Snapshotting
- Online scrub to fix issues

When you look at organizations that use btrfs in production, which includes Facebook and TripAdvisor among others, you will understand the importance of including it in this book.

In many ways, the btrfs filesystem was born from the failing of the ReiserFS file system after it lost its lead developer, Hans Reiser. Chris Mason, who had helped develop ReiserFS before moving on to SUSE, was hired by Oracle to develop high-end filesystems. This was the start of btrfs.

Overview of the lab environment

The Red Hat Enterprise Linux 7.1 virtual machine we will use for this book will have additional drives added for this section. Currently, we will use three disks:

- /dev/sda: This disk is used by the root filesystem
- /dev/sdb: This disk is used to house the yum repository
- /dev/sdc: This disk is used as the iSCSI LUN store

To demonstrate some key features of `btrfs`, we will add four additional virtual disks to the system so that we can use them while demonstrating the `btrfs` filesystem. Feel free to do the same if you are using a virtualized system. The different drives that we will add are as follows:

- `/dev/sdd`
- `/dev/sde`
- `/dev/sdf`
- `/dev/sdg`

Using the `lsblk` command on the demonstration system, you will be able to view the starting configuration that we will use from this point onward, as shown in the following screenshot:

```
[andrew@redhat7 Desktop]$ lsblk
NAME             MAJ:MIN RM    SIZE RO TYPE MOUNTPOINT
sda               8:0     0    10G   0 disk
├─sda1            8:1     0   500M   0 part /boot
└─sda2            8:2     0   9.5G   0 part
  ├─rhel-swap 253:0       0     1G   0 lvm  [SWAP]
  └─rhel-root 253:1       0   8.5G   0 lvm  /
sdb               8:16    0     6G   0 disk
└─sdb1            8:17    0     6G   0 part /repo
sdc               8:32    0     2G   0 disk
├─sdc1            8:33    0     1K   0 part
└─sdc5            8:37    0   200M   0 part
  └─iscsi-web 253:2       0   100M   0 lvm
sdd               8:48    0     1G   0 disk
sde               8:64    0     1G   0 disk
sdf               8:80    0     1G   0 disk
sdg               8:96    0     1G   0 disk
sr0              11:0     1  1024M   0 rom
```

Installing btrfs

Using Red Hat Enterprise Linux 7 or later, you will find that `btrfs` is installed by default even on a minimal installation. However, if you are using earlier versions, you can install the `btrfs` filesystem with yum in the normal way, as shown in the following command:

```
# yum install -y btrfs-progs
```

With the filesystem installed, we can check the version that we have implemented using the following command:

```
$ btrfs --version
```

On RHEL 7, the version is 3.12, whereas on RHEL 7.1, the version is 3.16.2.

Now that we understand a little of the power behind btrfs, let's begin with some simple implementation examples.

Creating the btrfs filesystem

To begin with, we will create a btrfs filesystem on the /dev/sdd complete disk. We do not need to partition the disk first, saving us time from the outset. This is shown in the following command line:

```
# mkfs.btrfs /dev/sdd
```

With the filesystem created, we can take the time to become familiar with the integrity check tool:

```
# btrfsck /dev/sdd
```

The following screenshot shows the output from my system:

```
[andrew@redhat7 ~]$ sudo btrfsck /dev/sdd
Checking filesystem on /dev/sdd
UUID: 646f6742-dc2a-41d5-a9f9-c26899c4de75
checking extents
checking free space cache
checking fs roots
checking csums
checking root refs
found 114688 bytes used err is 0
total csum bytes: 0
total tree bytes: 114688
total fs tree bytes: 32768
total extent tree bytes: 16384
btree space waste bytes: 108891
file data blocks allocated: 0
 referenced 0
Btrfs v3.16.2
```

To verify that the `btrfs` filesystem is in operation, we will create a directory and mount it therein. We will also copy some data and display the usage information for the disk:

```
# mkdir -p /data/simple
# mount /dev/sdd /data/simple
# find /usr/share/doc -name '*.pdf' -exec cp {} /data/simple \;
# btrfs filesystem show /dev/sdd
```

The output from the final command is shown in the following screenshot. We can see that we have 5.96 MiB of file space used:

```
[root@redhat7 ~]# btrfs filesystem show /dev/sdd
 Label: none   uuid: 646f6742-dc2a-41d5-a9f9-c26899c4de75
         Total devices 1 FS bytes used 5.96MiB
         devid    1 size 1.00GiB used 138.38MiB path /dev/sdd

Btrfs v3.16.2
```

The additional space used (which shows as `138.38MiB`) includes typical metadata related to any filesystem, but additionally, by default, the `btrfs` filesystem stores free space information on the disk so that it's quick to retrieve it rather than searching the disk. This is controlled through the `space_cache` mount option, which is set by default. If you would like to disable this feature, use the `nospace_cache` mount option.

The Copy-On-Write technology

One of the underpinning technologies that helps with the success of the `btrfs` filesystem is **Copy-On-Write (CoW)**. CoW is used in logical volume management filesystems, including **ZFS** used in Solaris (an Oracle product), Microsoft's **Volume Shadow Copy**, and `btrfs`.

These CoW filesystems allow you to take instant snapshots or backups. This is due to the fact that as a file is written and a copy of it is made; hence, Copy-on-Write. As traditional filesystems implement this, the virtual disk technology can also implement this CoW technology in qcow2. In this way, any allocated disk space in the qcow2 disk file is not used on the host until it's written to.

For generic filesystems, you will find the CoW technology very useful. Being able to revert to previous file versions is like gold dust on traditional file servers. However, if you use `btrfs` to host very large data files, such as virtual disk files, the CoW technology can perform slow writes.

Using the `chattr` command in Linux, we can set or change the attributes of files and/or directories. Supported for `btrfs` filesystems, there is a file attribute to disable CoW. This attribute is useful only when it is set on an empty file. To ensure its effectiveness, we generally set this on a directory, so that all the files inherit this attribute at the time of file creation. The following commands show how to achieve this:

```
# mkdir /data/simple/cow
# chattr +C /data/simple/cow
# lsattr -d /data/simple/cow
# touch /data/simple/cow/vdisk1
# lsattr /data/simple/cow/vdisk1
```

In the following screenshot, we can see that creating a new file will automatically assign the `NoDataCoW` option. It does not matter how this file was created:

```
[root@redhat7 ~]# mkdir /data/simple/cow
[root@redhat7 ~]# chattr +C /data/simple/cow
[root@redhat7 ~]# lsattr /data/simple/cow
[root@redhat7 ~]# lsattr -v /data/simple/cow
[root@redhat7 ~]# lsattr -d /data/simple/cow
--------------C /data/simple/cow
[root@redhat7 ~]# touch /data/simple/cow/vdisk1
[root@redhat7 ~]# lsattr  /data/simple/cow
--------------C /data/simple/cow/vdisk1
[root@redhat7 ~]# 
```

Resizing btrfs filesystems

With `btrfs`, it's possible to resize the `btrfs` filesystem when it is online and is being accessed by users. The size of a filesystem will grow automatically if we add or remove devices; we will see this in the next subsection of this chapter; however; we can resize the filesystem should we need to even on a single device that we have created. Using the following command, we will shrink the assigned space to the filesystem by 500MiB:

```
# btrfs filesystem resize -500m /data/simple
```

If we check the size of the filesystem before and after, we can see the dynamic change that takes place:

```
[root@redhat7 ~]# df -hT
Filesystem            Type      Size  Used Avail Use% Mounted on
/dev/mapper/rhel-root xfs       8.5G  3.4G  5.1G  40% /
devtmpfs              devtmpfs  908M     0  908M   0% /dev
tmpfs                 tmpfs     917M  148K  917M   1% /dev/shm
tmpfs                 tmpfs     917M  8.9M  908M   1% /run
tmpfs                 tmpfs     917M     0  917M   0% /sys/fs/cgroup
/dev/sdb1             btrfs     6.0G  3.8G  1.7G  69% /repo
/dev/sda1             xfs       497M  124M  374M  25% /boot
/dev/sdd              btrfs     1.0G  6.1M  888M   1% /data/simple
[root@redhat7 ~]# btrfs filesystem resize -500m /data/simple
Resize '/data/simple' of '-500m'
[root@redhat7 ~]# df -hT
Filesystem            Type      Size  Used Avail Use% Mounted on
/dev/mapper/rhel-root xfs       8.5G  3.4G  5.1G  40% /
devtmpfs              devtmpfs  908M     0  908M   0% /dev
tmpfs                 tmpfs     917M  148K  917M   1% /dev/shm
tmpfs                 tmpfs     917M  8.9M  908M   1% /run
tmpfs                 tmpfs     917M     0  917M   0% /sys/fs/cgroup
/dev/sdb1             btrfs     6.0G  3.8G  1.7G  69% /repo
/dev/sda1             xfs       497M  124M  374M  25% /boot
/dev/sdd              btrfs     524M  6.1M  388M   2% /data/simple
```

Adding devices to the btrfs filesystem

We have already seen a little of volume management using LVM when we looked at iSCSI in *Chapter 4, Implementing iSCSI SANs,* and it's not exactly simple.

Volume management the old way

The following commands are used in order to manage the disk volumes in the old, traditional way:

```
# pvcreate /dev/sde1
# vgextend vg1 /dev/sde1
# lvextend -L+1000M /dev/vg1/data_lv
# resize2fs /dev/vg1/data
```

Volume management with btrfs

To start with, we will return the volume back to its original size before we add the second disk. Using the max option, we will ensure that the btrfs filesystem uses the maximum space available on the single disk we have in place so far:

```
# btrfs filesystem resize max /data/simple
```

In LVM and traditional filesystems, there were a total of four commands to be executed. In btrfs, we can perform this with a single command:

```
# btrfs device add /dev/sde /data/simple
```

This is all we need to do. The device is added and the filesystem is automatically increased to the available maximum space. We can use the btrfs filesystem show command against either /dev/sdd or /sdv/sde because both devices will hold a copy of the metadata by default. In the following commands, we can see that this in place and the screenshot will reinforce this message:

```
# btrfs filesystem show /dev/sdd
```

```
# df -hT /data/simple
```

After reviewing the following screenshot, we can see the command and output that is generated:

```
[root@redhat7 ~]# btrfs filesystem show /dev/sdd
Label: none   uuid: 646f6742-dc2a-41d5-a9f9-c26899c4de75
        Total devices 2 FS bytes used 5.96MiB
        devid    1 size 1.00GiB used 138.38MiB path /dev/sdd
        devid    2 size 1.00GiB used 0.00 path /dev/sde

Btrfs v3.16.2
[root@redhat7 ~]# df -hT /data/simple
Filesystem      Type   Size  Used Avail Use% Mounted on
/dev/sdd        btrfs  2.0G  6.1M  1.9G   1% /data/simple
```

Having the metadata stored on both devices allow for fault-tolerance and weakens the device to be queried:

```
# btrfs fi show /dev/sdd
```

```
# btrfs filesystem show /dev/sde
```

[Note that some subcommands can be shortened; in this case, fi is equivalent to filesystem.]

Balancing the btrfs filesystem

If the need to add the additional disk to the volume was due to it running out of disk space, then we may choose to help performance by spreading the data across both devices. This is achieved using the `balance` subcommand:

```
# btrfs filesystem balance start -d -m /data/simple
```

The `-m` argument represents metadata and `-d` represents data. In this way, the disks are used at an equal ratio.

The output from the demonstration system is shown in the following command; note that you can omit `filesystem` from the `balance` subcommand because it's optional in this case:

```
[root@redhat7 ~]# btrfs balance start -d -m /data/simple
Done, had to relocate 5 out of 5 chunks
[root@redhat7 ~]#
```

Mounting multidisk btrfs volumes from /etc/fstab

If we are mounting the `btrfs` volumes from the `/etc/fstab` file, we need to ensure that a `btrfs` scan is effected before we mount the `/data/simple` directory. This will locate all the devices that participate within the volume. The `initramfs` file system can complete this task for us on a later system including RHEL 7. If your existing filesystem was already using `btrfs`, the scan will be built-in your current `initramfs`. If `btrfs` is new to your system, you will need to generate a new initial RAM disk. Make sure that you use the correct `initramfs` and kernel version for your system when running the following command:

```
# dracut -v -a btrfs -f /boot/initramfs-$(uname -r) /boot/vmlinuz-$(uname -r)
```

We can then add an entry into the `/etc/fstab` file similar to the following:

```
/dev/sdd  /data/simple  btrfs  defaults  0 0
```

Creating a RAID1 mirror

The **RAID (Redundant Array of Inexpensive Disks)** software is also supported by `btrfs`. The following are the currently supported RAID levels:

- **RAID 0**: Striping without redundancy
- **RAID 1**: Disk mirroring
- **RAID 10**: Striped mirror

Currently, we have a multidisk `btrfs` filesystem, but without fault-tolerance. The implementation we used is RAID 0 / striping without parity. We can convert this to a RAID 1 system and mirror the metadata and the filesystem data as follows:

```
# btrfs balance start -dconvert=raid1 -mconvert=raid1 /data/simple
```

As you can see from the preceding command, the metadata and the filesystem data are converted to the software mirror of RAID 1.

We can create a mirrored device using `btrfs` from the outset easily and quickly. Mirroring does not give us extra disk space, but this does provide great fault-tolerance if the worst happens and we experience a disk failure. We can demonstrate this on our demonstration system using the extra disk that we have not used so far:

```
# mkfs.btrfs -m raid1 -d raid1 /dev/sdf /dev/sdg
# mkdir /data/mirror
# mount /dev/sdg /data/mirror
```

To create a mirror, we will use RAID1 for the metadata and the `-m` and `-d` data, as we did in the preceding convert example. The disk space available is 1 GB. Whatever we write to `/dev/sdf` is mirrored to `/dev/sdg`; with mirror, we lose 50 percent of the data storage, but have a high level of redundancy. We will similarly need to add an entry to the `/etc/fstab` file to ensure that the raid system mounts correctly at boot time. As `initramfs` now supports `btrfs` by running the device scan for us, there is no requirement to create `initramfs` at this stage:

```
/dev/sdf  /data/mirror  btrfs  defaults  0 0
```

Displaying the free disk space with standard tools—such as `df`—will not supply correct information; we need to use `btrfs` tools. The following command will list the free space available to the `/data/mirror` mount point:

```
# btrfs fi df /data/mirror
```

The output from the command is shown in the following screenshot:

```
[root@redhat7 ~]# btrfs fi df /data/mirror
Data, RAID1: total=893.62MiB, used=192.00KiB
Data, single: total=8.00MiB, used=0.00
System, RAID1: total=8.00MiB, used=16.00KiB
System, single: total=4.00MiB, used=0.00
Metadata, RAID1: total=102.38MiB, used=112.00KiB
Metadata, single: total=8.00MiB, used=0.00
GlobalReserve, single: total=16.00MiB, used=0.00
```

I know that we risk 7 years of bad luck even talking about it; however, mirrors can break. Part of the reason to create a mirror is to provide fault-tolerance. This is in itself an acceptance that hard disks can and do fail.

For this demonstration, we will destroy the /data/simple/ volume and reuse the devices that we employed for the simple volume. To destroy the btrfs metadata, the preferred utility is wipefs, which is part of the util-linux package. Firstly, we need to run the wipefs command against the disk or partition we need to wipe and then use the offset value with the -o option. Take a look at how we can wipe /dev/sdd and /dev/sde:

```
# umount /data/simple
# wipefs /dev/sdd
# wipefs -o 0x10040 /dev/sdd
# wipefs /dev/sde
# wipefs -o 0x10040 /dev/sde
```

The output from the first drive is listed for convenience in the following screenshot; the sequence is repeated from the second drive. Do not forget to remove the entry from the /etc/fstab file:

```
[root@redhat7 ~]# wipefs /dev/sdd
offset               type
----------------------------------------------------------------
0x10040              btrfs   [filesystem]
                     UUID:   646f6742-dc2a-41d5-a9f9-c26899c4de75

[root@redhat7 ~]# wipefs -o 0x10040 /dev/sdd
/dev/sdd: 8 bytes were erased at offset 0x00010040 (btrfs): 5f 42 48 52 66 53 5f 4d
```

With these disks wiped, we can reuse them in other arrays.

We will add data to the mirror volume in the same way that we did with the simple volume. In this way, we can be sure that data stays intact:

```
# find /usr/share/doc -name '*.pdf' -exec cp {} /data/mirror \;
```

We will unmount the mirror volume now and emulate the failure of one of the disks as follows:

```
# umount /data/mirror
# wipefs -o 0x10040 /dev/sdg
```

We will now experience a problem when we try to remount the mirror volume using the mount command, and we will have to mount the mirror volume using the -o degraded option:

```
# mount -o degraded /dev/sdf /data/mirror
```

At this stage, our data is available, so we can breathe a sigh of relief:

```
# ls /data/mirror
```

We still have a RAID 1 array and the minimum number of members for this is two, so we need to add a new device as follows:

```
# btrfs device add /dev/sdd /data/mirror
```

We can now remove the failed or missing device:

```
# btrfs device delete missing /data/mirror
```

The missing keyword will search for the first missing member in the array. We can then delete this device. The RAID 1 array is now fully operational, provisioning software mirroring across two devices again.

Using btrfs snapshots

Hopefully, what you have seen so far in btrfs will be of interest, but, of course, there is always much more to see and learn. We will now look at snapshots. Btrfs snapshots can be used as read-only or read/write copies of your data. With btrfs as a Copy-on-Write-based filesystem, there is no need to copy large amounts of data across because we only need to copy the data when it changes. In the meantime, the original data is linked to the new location. In this way, a snapshot of a large filesystem can be taken instantly. Snapshots can be put to use in a couple of ways:

- As part of a backup solution where you may be concerned with open files affecting the backup; the snapshot will be created as read-only. Subsequently, you will implement a backup of the snapshot. In this way, the backup will be of the host filesystem at the point in time that the snapshot was created.

- Snapshots can be useful where you feel that rolling back to the original data may be useful, perhaps in a testing environment where you need to implement many changes and easily be able to restore back to the original data very quickly.

Btrfs snapshots rely on subvolumes; source and destination subvolumes need to be within the same filesystem. If you'll recall the data is just linked until it's changed; this is handled in the same way as traditional hard links.

Subvolumes within the btrfs filesystem are discrete management identities, which allow more granular control of elements of a single filesystem. We will begin by creating a single subvolume so that we may gain a little understanding of this technology before creating snapshots. We will re-employ the /dev/sde disk to be mounted as our simple volume and start by reformatting the mirror volume:

```
# mkfs.btrfs /dev/sde
# mount /dev/sde /data/simple
```

At this stage, the complete filesystem for /dev/sde is available and mounted at the /data/simple directory. There is no data stored here yet, but we effectively have a single view of the filesystem with the simple directory. Subvolumes allow you to view the same filesystem in different ways by mounting elements of the filesystem (subvolumes) to the directories that we choose and with selected mount options appropriate for the data.

We will create a new subvolume after the existing /data/simple directory:

```
# btrfs subvolume create /data/simple/vol1
```

The output is quite minimal, as shown in the following screenshot:

```
[root@redhat7 ~]# btrfs subvolume create /data/simple/vol1
Create subvolume '/data/simple/vol1'
```

We can list the subvolumes, as shown in the following command and screenshot:

```
# btrfs subvolume list /data/simple
# ls /data/simple
```

The following screenshot shows the output of the preceding command:

```
[root@redhat7 ~]# btrfs subvolume list /data/simple/
ID 256 gen 6 top level 5 path vol1
[root@redhat7 ~]# ls /data/simple/
vol1
```

We can also see that creating the subvolume also created the directory within the filesystem itself. We will not be able to remove the directory from the filesystem because this is not only a directory, but also a subvolume. To delete a directory, you will need to delete the subvolume.

We won't delete the directory, but should we need to delete it at a later stage, the command to delete it will be as follows:

```
# btrfs subvolume delete /data/simple/vol1
```

This will delete the subvolume along with the directory in very much the same way as creating the subvolume also created the directory within the filesystem.

We will now add some data to the subvolume; if you did delete it, you can simply recreate it again. We can copy the PDF files that we have become familiar with to this volume:

```
# cp /data/mirror/* /data/simple/vol1
```

If we need to make this data available elsewhere, we can mount the subvolume wherever we need and with mount options that we feel appropriate. For example, we have documentation in this directory so that we can mount it as read-only in another directory:

```
# mount -o ro,subvol=vol1 /dev/sde /mnt
```

At the root of the /mnt mount point, we will see the PDF files we added to the vol1 directory. They are still available in the original location under /data/simple/vol1. In this way, we can control access to the data from how it's mounted.

Now that we have some knowledge of subvolumes, we will investigate snapshots. The snapshot must be created in the same filesystem as the target data; as we mentioned before, the instant generation of a snapshot is affected by a form of internal linking within the filesystem.

We will generate the snapshot of the existing `voll` data and also specify the option `-r` to ensure that the backup is read-only. In this way, we can return to this *point in time* backup by copying the data back from the `backup` directory. No additional disk space is used unless the original data is changed:

```
# btrfs subvolume snapshot -r /data/simple/voll/ /data/simple/backup
```

We can list the subvolumes easily using the following command:

```
# btrfs subvolume list /data/simple
```

We may base the backup scenario around the fact that the documentation may be written too frequently. Also, we want a solution to be able to recover from poorly executed edits quickly.

To create a read-only snapshot of the working subvolume, use the following command:

```
# btrfs subvolume snapshot -r /data/simple/voll /data/simple/backup/
```

Listing the contents of the working directory and the backup directory should reveal that the contents are the same:

```
# ls /data/simple/voll
```

```
# ls /data/simple/backup
```

The name `backup` is not important, but useful in the context of its use. As always, a good naming scheme can help understand the directory's purpose unlike the name we gave to `voll`.

Should we accidently delete all the files from `/data/simple/voll`, the CoW technology in `btrfs` will then write the changed data to the backup snapshot: `/data/simple/backup`. This will also be the case if the files were modified in any way rather than deleted; the snapshot holds files as they were at the time the snapshot was created. We can simply copy the files back to the original location in the event of a catastrophe.

For the moment, we will look at how to delete this snapshot. Later in this chapter, we will see how to use snapper as a simple mechanism in order to manage snapshots on LVM and `btrfs` systems:

```
# btrfs subvolume delete /data/simple/backup
```

Optimizing btrfs for solid state drives

When creating a `btrfs` filesystem on multiple SSDs, using the single `-m` option will ensure that the metadata is not duplicated. On an SSD, duplicating metadata is thought of as a waste of space and has an overhead that can lessen the life of the disk, as shown in the following code:

```
# mkfs.btrfs -m single /dev/sdb
```

The second way is to use the `ssd` mount option. This option will set a few performance options:

- Allows large metadata clusters
- Allows more sequential data allocation
- Disables leaf writing to match key and block order in the b-tree database
- Commits b-tree log fragments without batching multiple processes

Managing snapshots with snapper

The snapshot command is included on RHEL 7 and can be used to manage snapshots and view their differences with the original data easily. It can be employed along with LVM or btrfs `systems.h`.

To install snapper, we fall back to RHEL's package management:

```
# yum install snapper
```

Currently, there seems to be a bug or feature on SELinux that prevents snapper from working if SELinux is enforced. We could allow the correct SELinux access to our resources by creating a new policy or simply set `snapperd_t` to a permissive domain. In this way, we can still use the power and security of SELinx, but just have it disabled for snapper as follows:

```
# semanage permissive -a snapperd_t
```

At a later date, you can use the `-d` option to delete the enabled snapper and the SELinux support:

```
# semanage permissive -d snapperd_t
```

For the moment, we will leave snapper in the permissive mode and proceed to create a configuration for snapper and our `/data/simple/vol1` data:

```
# snapper -c simple_data create-config -f btrfs /data/simple/
```

Using the following command, we can list the configurations that we have:

```
# snapper list-configs
```

The following screenshot shows the creation of the configuration and the listing command:

```
[root@redhat7 ~]# snapper -c simple_data create-config -f btrfs /data/simple/vol1
[root@redhat7 ~]# snapper list-configs
Config     | Subvolume
-----------+------------------
simple_data | /data/simple/vol1
[root@redhat7 ~]#
```

Creating the configuration will create a hidden directory .snapshots at the root /data/simple/vol1 directory. The configuration itself is stored in /etc/snapper/ configs; a log file exits from troubleshooting located at /var/log/snapper.log.

Now that we have the foundation created, we will create the snapshot:

```
# snapper --config simple_data create --description "Start"
```

We can see that the process is very easy, quick, and saves us a lot of effort. If we check the subvolumes that now exits after /data/simple, we will see .snapshots and the numbered subvolume after this:

```
# btrfs subvolume list /data/simple
```

The output is shown in the following screenshot:

```
[root@redhat7 ~]# snapper --config simple_data create --description "Start"
[root@redhat7 ~]# btrfs subvolume list /data/simple/
ID 257 gen 26 top level 5 path vol1
ID 263 gen 27 top level 257 path vol1/.snapshots
ID 264 gen 26 top level 263 path vol1/.snapshots/1/snapshot
[root@redhat7 ~]#
```

More easily and normally though, we use snapper entirely to manage this, and we should view snapshots with the following command:

```
# snapper --config simple_data list
```

To show how we can view the difference in data, we will delete a PDF file from the original vol1 location:

```
# rm /data/simple/vol1/tutorial.pdf
```

With this file removed, we will now have a difference between the original data and the snapshot. The CoW system will have the deleted file written to the snapshot location as the deletion occurred. We can view the difference in the data using the following command, where 0 is the original data and 1 is the snapshot:

```
# snapper -c simple_data status 0..1
```

The output of the command is shown in the following screenshot, which indicates that the snapshot has the extra file now:

```
[root@redhat7 ~]# snapper -c simple_data status 0..1
+..... /data/simple/vol1/tutorial.pdf
[root@redhat7 ~]# █
```

To restore the deleted file, we will use the undochange command; note that we need to display the effect from the snapshot, to the original or 1..0, as shown in the following command:

```
# snapper -c simple_data undochange 1..0
```

We now have the tutorial.pdf file returned to us in the vol1 directory as follows:

```
# ls /data/simple/vol1/tutorial.pdf
```

From the following screenshot, you will be able to see the file restore command and the listing of the returned file:

```
[root@redhat7 ~]# snapper -c simple_data undochange 1..0
create:1 modify:0 delete:0
[root@redhat7 ~]# ls /data/simple/vol1/tutorial.pdf
/data/simple/vol1/tutorial.pdf
[root@redhat7 ~]# █
```

Summary

In this chapter, we saw the power that can be unleashed with the `btrfs` filesystem and the time we can save using it compared with other Linux logical volume systems such as LVM. We also saw how to implement software RAID and then combined the file management, logical volume management, and RAID management to a single command.

Using snapper to help manage snapshots works well for us on LVM and `btrfs` systems. We used snapper with the `btrfs` filesystem in this chapter.

In the next chapter, we will see how to share files on the network using **NFS (Network File System)**, the traditional UNIX way to share file resources on your network.

6
File Sharing with NFS

File sharing with **Network File System (NFS)** is the traditional way on Unix and Linux for remote hosts to be able to mount filesystems over a network and interact with them as if they were mounted locally. Although RHEL 7 supports both NFSv3 and NFSv4, there is no longer any support for NFSv2. The RHEL 7 client will default to NFSv4 and falls back to NFSv3 if a connection cannot be established. Using NFSv4 simplifies location of services behind a firewall with only the TCP port 2049 required for client access; however, we will demonstrate both the NFSv4 and v3 firewall configurations. During this chapter, the following topics will be covered:

- Overview of NFS
- Overview of the lab environment
- The NFS server configuration
- Using exportfs
- Hosting NFSv4 behind a firewall
- Hosting NFSv3 behind a firewall
- The NFS client configuration
- Auto-mounting NFS with autofs

An overview of NFS

We have been used to NFSv4 being included with Red Hat Enterprise Linux 6. RHEL 7 includes additional support for pNFS (Parallel NFS) with NFSv4.1. pNFS, providing security and performance enhancements, which allow more efficient connections to clients behind firewalls and **Network Address Translation (NAT)** routers.

Support for NFSv2 is no longer available, which is no great loss, as it did not support file sizes above 2 GB and was not as robust as version 3 and 4.

Using NFSv4, mounting and locking protocols are incorporated in a *batteries included* philosophy. This allows the use of just the one TCP port: 2049. However, with NFSv3, we have to use rpcbind and set static ports for additional services so that a firewall can be configured. This simplifies the firewall configuration, which you will see later, as access only to the TCP port 2049 is required.

Both the server and client tools are installed together from the nfs-utils package. This package includes tools for both the NFSv4 and V3 protocols. It also includes other useful tools such as nfsiostat that can be used to monitor NFS shares usage on an NFS server. To list the contents of an installed package, you can use the rpm command, as shown in the following command lines that can be run as a standard user:

```
$ rpm -ql nfs-utils #lists all files in the package
$ rpm -qd nfs-utils #lists just the documentation files
$ rpm -qc nfs-utils #list only the configuration files
$ rpm -qi nfs-utils #displays descriptive information on the package
```

Overview of the lab environment

For demonstrations is this chapter, we will use two virtual machines running in an **Oracle VirtualBox** virtualization environment. VirtualBox can be downloaded from https://www.virtualbox.org/ free of charge and is available for Windows, Mac OS X, Linux, and Solaris hosts.

The NFS Server will be configured on the RHEL 7.1 host with the IP address of 192.168.10.10 and the hostname of nfshost. The NFS client will be configured on the RHEL 7.1 host with the IP address of 192.168.10.11 and the hostname of nfsclient.

Both machines were installed with a minimal configuration; we have installed the nfs-utils package on both hosts, as shown in the following code:

```
$ sudo yum install -y nfs-utils
```

Additionally, on the nfshost host, we have installed the net-tools package so that we can display open ports with the netstat command. The command to install net-tools is as follows:

```
$ sudo yum install -y net-tools
```

The firewall is running the default setup and is managed with the `firewall-cmd` command. To allow NFSv4 connections to `nfshost`, we have additionally opened the TCP port `2049` using the following commands:

```
$ sudo firewall-cmd --add-port=2049/tcp --permanent
$ sudo firewall-cmd --reload
```

 We will cover more on firewall on RHEL 7 later in this chapter and also look at how to use the `firewall-cmd` and `firewalld` service in detail in *Chapter 11, Network Security with firewalld*, of this book.

NFS not only uses a firewall to protect the server, but also supports TCP wrappers to control access. The rights to access a service can be determined by the use of the `/etc/hosts.allow` and `/etc/hosts.deny` files.

The NFS server configuration

To configure the NFS server, we choose which directories we want to share. The terminology used in NFS to share a directory is *to export* the directory; therefore, shared directories are known as **exports**.

To permanently export a directory, we add the configuration to the `/etc/exports` file. This file exists, but will be empty on a new system. The `nfs-server` service will read this file on startup to determine which directories should be available to the network client. If `/etc/exports` is changed, reloading the `nfs-server` service will force the service to reread the file, as shown in the following command line:

```
$ sudo systemctl reload nfs-server
```

To display the current exports on the server, we can use the `exportfs` or `showmount` command. We will now take a little time to start the required services and create our first simple export.

Firstly, we will need to start the required services. We can start and enable each service independently, but in the spirit of automation, we will write a simple loop at Command Prompt to save some typing and time. We will use `sudo`; your user account will need to be listed within the `sudoers` file. Once you are sure that you have access to `sudo`, the command will be executed as follows:

```
for s in rpcbind nfs-server nfs-lock nfs-idmap ; do
    sudo systemctl enable $s
    sudo systemctl start $s
done
```

If it makes the syntax clearer to you, the following screenshot shows the command as executed on `nfshost`:

```
[vagrant@nfshost ~]$ for s in "rpcbind nfs-server nfs-lock nfs-idmap" ; do
> sudo systemctl enable $s
> sudo systemctl start $s
> done
```

Simple exports

Without editing the `/etc/exports` file, we cannot export anything on the filesystem. As a result, there will be no output when we display the local exports using `exportfs`, as shown in the following command line:

```
$ sudo exportfs
```

We will have little luck with the `showmount` command, as shown in the following screenshot:

```
[vagrant@nfshost ~]$ showmount -e
Export list for nfshost:
```

As you can see, the `showmount` command will show the export list heading, but, of course, the list is empty until we explicitly define some exported directories.

> The `showmount` command can be used on remote hosts, such as the `nfsclient`, to list exported directories, but this will depend on additional services. So, the firewall on `nfshost` will need to be configured for NFSv3. We will discuss this later in this chapter.

I accept that sharing nothing, nada, zilch is not the most exciting feature that you will find in this book, at least we have discovered some useful tools such as `exportfs` and `showmount`. We will now export an existing directory just to get used to NFS. To do this, we will need to edit as root the `/etc/exports` file; we can do this using `sudo`. You can log in as root directly or with the `su` command. We will add the following line to export or share the `/usr/share/doc` directory. This is just a simple test. We will add our own directories and content later. For our demonstration, we will stick to using `vi` in order to edit the file; however, you are welcome to use your favorite editor:

```
$ sudo vi /etc/exports
```

With the file open and without the contents on a new NFS server, we can add the following line to export the /usr/share/doc directory:

```
/usr/share/doc *(ro)
```

Using the cat command, we can show the filename that we should be editing and the files' content once the edit is complete, as shown in the following screenshot:

```
[vagrant@nfshost ~]$ cat /etc/exports
/usr/share/doc *(ro)
```

Having exported a directory, we should be able to see this using exportfs or showmount.

 The exportfs command requires administrative access, whereas showmount does not.

However, before we get ahead of ourselves, we need to recall that the nfs-server service reads this file when it starts up and is currently running. We can restart this service, but it will be better to reload the service. In this way, there is no need to bring the service down if the remote hosts currently have mounted exports. Running the following command will reload the service and then display the exports directory or directories:

```
$ sudo systemctl reload nfs-server
$ sudo exportfs
```

The output from both commands previously listed is now displayed in the following screenshot:

```
[vagrant@nfshost ~]$ sudo systemctl restart nfs-server
[vagrant@nfshost ~]$ sudo exportfs
/usr/share/doc   <world>
```

When we defined exports, we exported a directory to all hosts denoted with an asterix symbol; any options for the export are included within parenthesis. We specified the export as read only with the inclusion of the ro option.

As a simple test, we can now use the nfsclient host to access this export. From the console of the nfsclient, we can access the exported directory and mount it to the local /mnt directory on the nfsclient using the following command:

```
$ sudo mount 192.168.10.10:/usr/share/doc /mnt
```

We can use either the IP address or the hostname of the server as long as the hostname is resolvable via DNS, **mDNS (Multicast DNS)**, or the localhost's file. The end of the server hostname or IP address must be denoted with a colon.

We can easily list the contents of the exported directory using the standard `ls` command against the /mnt directory. The truncated output from the ls command is shown in the following screenshot:

```
[vagrant@nfsclient ~]$ ls /mnt
acl-2.2.51                    libproxy-0.4.11
aic94xx-firmware-30           libpwquality-1.2.3
alsa-firmware-1.0.27          libquadmath-4.8.2
alsa-lib-1.0.27.2             libquadmath-devel-4.8.2
alsa-tools-1.0.27             libsoup-2.42.2
apr-1.4.8                     libss-1.42.9
```

Advanced exports

We have seen how simple life can be for a Linux system administrator if only simple exporting of directories is all that is needed. However, although this option may fit some directory exports and servers, others may require a little more time and effort.

The basic directive within the /etc/exports file is as follows:

export host(options)

The structure of these variables is as follows:

- `export`: This is the directory on the NFS server being exported or shared
- `host`: This is the host or network to which the exported directory is shared
- `options`: These are specific options to be used by a host or network that proceeds the parenthesis

It's also possible to write a single entry to share one export with different options to different hosts or networks, as shown in the following example code:

export host(options) host(options)

Expanding this to actual values in place of the variables a working example to allow read/write access to 192.168.10.11 but read-only access to all other hosts, we can examine the following code:

/usr/share/doc *(ro) 192.168.10.11(rw,sync)

Options are comma-separated, and we have additionally added the `sync` option in the options for the `nfsclient 192.168.10.11`. The `sync` option will ensure that writes to this export are written to disk on demand, rather than waiting for write-buffers to be flushed to the disk. Linux uses a system of buffering that promotes the use of dirty-cache buffers. These are written to disk as numbers grow. The `sync` option ensures that these buffers are written to the disk immediately. This has a negative impact on performance, but can be more reliable as connections are not always maintained.

If a single line in the `/etc/exports` file becomes too long, then it can be wrapped using the backslash (\) character. Within a file, each export must be represented with its own individual line. Additional blank lines are ignored and can be added for readability. Lines may be configured to be ignored by the server if they are commented with the line starting with the hash (#) character.

> If the read/write access is granted to the export and the filesystem is read only to the user, they still have read-only access. If the export is set to read only and the filesystem would normally allow read and write access to the user, they still have read-only access. Quite simply, when combining file and export permissions, the most restrictive permission is effective.

If we are to be 100 percent accurate, the options for an export are optional. If an option is not set, the default option will apply. We can then rewrite the previous example making use of the defaults as follows:

```
/usr/share/doc * 192.168.10.11(rw)
```

From the modified example, you should be able to guess correctly that the `ro` and `sync` default options are no longer explicitly set, but they will still be effective. The effective options for an exported directory can be seen using the `exportfs` command with the `-v` option, as show in the following command:

```
$ sudo exportfs -v
```

If an option is not set and displayed in the output of the previous command, then you will see the default option.

The default options for the NFS server include the following; more details can be found on the `man` page:

- `ro`: This makes the exported filesystem as read only on the remote host.
- `sync`: The NFS server writes changes to the disk before responding to new requests.

- `wdelay`: This is used with the `sync` option; the NFS server will delay writing to the disk and more writes are anticipated imminently.

- `root_squash`:The remote users connecting as root or `UID 0` are changed to `nfsnobody` and as such, we will only be able to collect permissions granted to others. This effectively squashes the permissions of root access remotes, preventing unauthorized root access to exported filesystems.

We will now amend the `/etc/exports` file to represent two sets of hosts that we will export to and verify that we can connect from the designated host `192.168.10.11`. The export is set to `rw`, which supersedes the `ro` option set to all hosts with `*`. We will use `echo` to overwrite the `exports` file so that you can see the edit being made through to the file along with other commands. These commands are listed in the following example with a supporting screenshot to display export options:

```
$ sudo bash -c 'echo "/usr/share/doc * 192.168.10.11(rw)" > /etc/exports'
$ sudo systemctl reload nfs-server
$ sudo exportfs -v
```

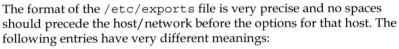

```
[vagrant@nfshost ~]$ sudo bash -c 'echo "/usr/share/doc * 192.168.10.11(rw)" > /etc/exports'
[vagrant@nfshost ~]$ sudo systemctl reload nfs-server
[vagrant@nfshost ~]$ sudo exportfs -v
/usr/share/doc  192.168.10.11(rw,wdelay,root_squash,no_subtree_check,sec=sys,rw,secure,root_squash,no
_all_squash)
/usr/share/doc  <world>(ro,wdelay,root_squash,no_subtree_check,sec=sys,ro,secure,root_squash,no_all_s
quash)
[vagrant@nfshost ~]$ []
```

From the preceding screenshot, we can see that the `192.168.10.11` host has read/write access, whereas `<world>` or all other hosts have read-only access.

Be cautious with spaces

The format of the `/etc/exports` file is very precise and no spaces should precede the host/network before the options for that host. The following entries have very different meanings:

```
/home server1(rw)
#correctly shares /home as read and write to server1
/home server1 (rw)
#shares the export /home to server1 using the default
read-only and to <world> read-write is assigned, the
asterisk can be omitted when designating all hosts.
```

Pseudo-root

As you can see in the /usr/share/doc current export, it's normal for the complete path of the exported directory to be used when accessing it on the server. It's possible to simplify paths that are needed to access exported directories using a pseudo-root directory on the server. This is only an option for NFSv4 servers and clients. With the pseudo-root directory in place, we can mount other directories to that path. Let's take a look at this on our nfshost.

We will clear the current exported directory. This time, we will set up sharing from scratch with a little thought and planning.

Firstly, we will create a new directory on nfshost that will act as the pseudo-root directory:

```
$ sudo mkdir -m 1777 /var/exports
```

We can create this directory and set mode or permissions at the same time. Here, we set permissions to all users and include the sticky bit so that users can only delete the files that they own.

Next, we will overwrite the current exports within the /etc/exports file with the newly created directory:

```
$ sudo bash -c 'echo "/var/exports 192.168.10.11(rw,fsid=0,crossmnt)" > /etc/exports'
$ sudo systemctl reload nfs-server
```

These commands are run on nfshost and shown in the following screenshot:

```
nfshost $ sudo bash -c 'echo "/var/exports 192.168.10.11(rw,fsid=0,crossmnt)" > /etc/exports'
nfshost $ sudo systemctl reload nfs-server
nfshost $ ▯
```

There are two new options that we implement here:

- fsid=0: This sets the directory as the root directory of the server when accessed over NFS. In this way, the /var/export directory is accessed from the remote client as 192.168.10.10:/.

- crossmnt: This is the clever option that we need in order to allow access to directories that are mounted underneath this mount point. To mount directories to this export, we will use the mount --bind command. This will be covered very shortly.

Setting the export option as read/write enables us to control access using file permissions on the `nfshost`. Any user will have full permission to the export when accessing from the `nfsclient`, so restrictions will need to be made in the filesystem.

With the NFS root in place, we can make any directory within the filesystem available after this entry point. We will need to create subdirectories as mount points within the `/var/exports` directory and then mount the local targets to these mount points. We will add a central shared directory called `/home/marketing` and mount this and the existing `/usr/share/doc` directory after the newly created `exports` directory. The commands to achieve this are shown in the following command lines:

```
$ sudo mkdir -m 1777 /home/marketing
$ touch /home/marketing/marketing.doc
$ sudo mkdir -m 777 /var/exports/{doc,marketing}
$ sudo mount --bind /usr/share/doc /var/exports/doc
$ sudo mount --bind /home/marketing /var/exports/marketing
```

The following bullet points explain the preceding command line steps:

- After working through the list of commands, we first create the central shared directory that we will add after the `/home` structure. This may be desired due to partitioning and quota settings that dictate that the marketing directory should be on the `/home` partition.
- We add a document to this directory so that we are able to view some content.
- The third command in the list creates both the doc and marketing directories. We will use these directories as mount points. These directories are created in the `/var/exports` NFS root.
- The final two commands mount the local directories to their export mount points. In this way, we can easily add any directory to be available directly after `/var/exports`.

Listing the contents on the `/var/exports/marketing` directory should show the file we created in the `/home/marketing` directory. Refer to the following screenshot:

```
[vagrant@nfshost ~]$ ls /var/exports/marketing/
marketing.doc
[vagrant@nfshost ~]$ 
```

In the same way, looking at the contents of `/var/exports/doc` should show the contents of `/usr/share/doc`.

For permanency of local mounts, we will need to add them to the /etc/fstab file in the following format:

```
/originaldir /newdir none bind
```

We will now edit the fstab file as root and add these two lines to the end of the file to ensure that the mount points are populated during boot:

```
/usr/share/doc /var/exports/doc none bind
/home/marketing /var/exports/marketing none bind
```

When you return to the nfsclient system, you will be able test both exports and permissions. The original /home/marketing directory is writable, whereas the /usr/share/doc directory is not:

From the nfsclient system we can issue the following commands:

```
$ sudo mount 192.168.10.10:/ /mnt
$ touch /mnt/marketing/file1
$ touch /mnt/doc/file1
```

Now the file path is simpler, being able to access both folders with a single path from the server's NFS root. We should also note that although the exported directory is read/ write, we can write to the marketing directory using the first touch command, but the second touch command will fail as the target filesystem is read only.

Using exportfs to create temporary exports

It's not always desirable to create permanent exports within the /etc/exports file. Should you want to define a new export temporarily, you can use the exportfs command. As we have already defined the NFS root to be /var/exports, all directories that we export must be after that structure. Let's temporarily export /var/export/doc to all hosts. We can do so using the following command:

```
$ sudo exportfs *:/var/exports/doc
```

On the next restart of nfs-server, this export will be lost; however, if you need to delete it ahead of this, you can implement the following command:

```
$ sudo exportfs -u *:/var/exports/doc
```

Should you need to include export options with the temporary export, use the `-o` option in a similar manner, as shown in the following command:

```
$ sudo exportfs *:/var/exports/doc -o ro,all_squash
```

To display the current exports, you can run `exportfs` by itself:

```
$ sudo exportfs
```

Hosting NFSv4 behind a firewall

When you access the NFS server using v4 of the protocol on both the client and server, the firewall configuration is quite simple with only the TCP port `2049` required to be opened. The default firewall daemon on RHEL 7 is `firewalld` and is managed from the command line using `firewall-cmd`.

We have been running the standard firewall for our demonstrations thus far just opening the one additional port `2049`, as detailed in the lab overview earlier in this section.

We can list the current firewall configuration using the following command:

```
$ sudo firewall-cmd --list-all
```

The output is shown in the following screenshot:

```
nfshost $ sudo firewall-cmd --list-all
public (default, active)
  interfaces: enp0s3 enp0s8
  sources:
  services: dhcpv6-client ssh
  ports: 2049/tcp
  masquerade: no
  forward-ports:
  icmp-blocks:
  rich rules:
```

Should you need to remove the port setting that we added, this can be done using the following commands:

```
$ sudo firewall-cmd --remove-port=2049/tcp --permanent
$ sudo firewall-cmd --reload
```

Of course, a client can no longer access the NFS exports. We have the choice of adding ports or service entries. To add a service entry, the port and associated service needs to be defined in the /etc/services file. This can be easily checked using the grep command. An example is shown in the following command:

```
$ grep 2049 /etc/services
```

We do have an entry for the port 2049 and the service is called nfs. To use the service name in the firewall configuration, you may use the following command:

```
$ sudo firewall-cmd --add-service=nfs --permanent
$ sudo firewall-cmd --reload
$ sudo firewall-cmd --list-all
```

This is illustrated with the following screenshot:

```
nfshost $ sudo firewall-cmd --add-service=nfs --permanent
success
nfshost $ sudo firewall-cmd --reload
success
nfshost $ sudo firewall-cmd --list-all
public (default, active)
  interfaces: enp0s3 enp0s8
  sources:
  services: dhcpv6-client nfs ssh
  ports:
  masquerade: no
  forward-ports:
  icmp-blocks:
  rich rules:
```

With the service now allowed in all firewall rules, we can continue to access the NFS export from nfsclient. If you want to use tools like showmount remotely or if you have NFSv3 clients, you will need to open more ports and set some ports statically.

Hosting NFSv3 behind a firewall

If we try to use the showmount command from the nfsclient, we should be able to list exports on the remote NFS server. The syntax will be as follows:

```
$ showmount -e 192.168.10.10
```

The command and the corresponding error are shown in the following screenshot:

```
[vagrant@nfsclient ~]$ showmount -e 192.168.10.10
clnt_create: RPC: Port mapper failure - Unable to receive: errno 113 (No route to host)
[vagrant@nfsclient ~]$ _
```

At this stage, we can choose from the following options:

- Pack our bags and go home, perhaps it will be better tomorrow
- Google the error
- Debug the error ourselves

Diagnosing NFSv3 issues

Now, Google is often really good at helping us, but you fail to learn fault-finding techniques, so let's opt out of option 3 and install the tcpdump command-line packet analyzer so that we can see what is happening. This can be installed on nfsclient using yum as follows:

```
$ sudo yum install -y tcpdump
```

To capture network traffic between the nfsclient and the nfshost and to print port numbers that are being accessed, we can use the following command:

```
$ sudo tcpdump -nn -i enp0s8 host 192.168.10.10
```

The options to tcpdump used here are listed as follows:

- -nn: This shows the host IP addresses and port numbers and not their names.
- -i: This is the interface to be used. You will need to use the correct interface name, where we have used enp0s8 as the interface we need to listen on.
- host 192.168.10.10: This displays traffic to and from this host. This is the IP address for the nfshost.

From another console or the SSH session, try the `showmount` command again. While viewing the console where `tcpdump` is running, we should try to access the UDP port `111` on the server twice and report the error. The output is shown from my system in the following screenshot:

```
[vagrant@nfsclient ~]$ sudo tcpdump -nn -i enp0s8 host 192.168.10.10
tcpdump: verbose output suppressed, use -v or -vv for full protocol decode
listening on enp0s8, link-type EN10MB (Ethernet), capture size 65535 bytes
16:54:18.566670 IP 192.168.10.11.60609 > 192.168.10.10.111: UDP, length 56
16:54:18.568174 IP 192.168.10.10 > 192.168.10.11: ICMP host 192.168.10.10 unreachable - admin prohibi
ted, length 92
16:54:18.568677 IP 192.168.10.11.41040 > 192.168.10.10.111: UDP, length 56
16:54:18.569184 IP 192.168.10.10 > 192.168.10.11: ICMP host 192.168.10.10 unreachable - admin prohibi
ted, length 92
```

The UDP Port `111` is not open in the firewall configuration of `nfshost`. If you recall, we have just displayed the allowed services and ports for the firewall and `111` was not among them.

Port `111` is held open by the `portmapper` service run by `rpcbind` and shows as the `sunrpc` service in the `/etc/services` file. We can check this by running `netstat` on the `nfshost` as follows:

`$ sudo netstat -aunp`

The options to `netstat` used here are listed as follows:

- `-a`: This shows all and by all; by this we mean listening and established ports
- `-u`: This displays UDP ports only
- `-n`: This displays port and network numbers rather than resolving them to names
- `-p`: This displays the process name holding the port or connection open

To use the `-p` option, we must run as root (using `sudo`); otherwise, the process column will be left blank.

The theory behind the `rpcbind` service is that it will return the port address so that the required service is running to the requesting client. This is how NFSv3 works and the `showmount` command still makes use of this old protocol. The incoming request from `showmount` from the remote client asks for the address of the NFS Mount Daemon. This is the service running as the process: `rpc.mountd`. These services can run on dynamically-assigned ports. As such, it requires further configuration to reliably have them allowed through your firewall on a long term basis.

The pictorial process of what should be happening with showmount starts with the request for the rpc.mountd port, as shown in the following screenshot:

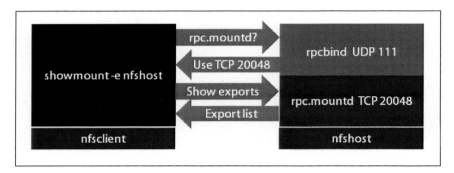

We can start by allowing the rpcbind traffic from the firewall to the nfshost:

```
$ sudo firewall-cmd --add-port=111/udp --permanent
$ sudo firewall-cmd --reload
```

> Don't forget to reload the firewall once you have added the port. It's all too easy to forget to complete this.

Now that we can connect to the rpcbind portmapper service running on the UDP port 111, we should go a little further. Remember that we are really trying to debug the process and learn some useful tcpdump analysis tricks. We can repeat the previous exercise running tcpdump on one console and showmount on the other (both consoles running on the nfsclient). The error reported from the showmount command should be slightly different now. To illustrate this, the following screenshot shows the current error, where we have the UDP port 111 open:

```
[vagrant@nfsclient ~]$ showmount -e 192.168.10.10
rpc mount export: RPC: Unable to receive; errno = No route to host
[vagrant@nfsclient ~]$
```

So, the error is slightly different now, we now no longer have the error number; however, we can see from the tcpdump output that we received the reply from the nfshost. Subsequently, we then try to make a TCP connection back to the host on the port 20048.

To identify the purpose of this port, we can again use `netstat`, but this time, we will replace `-u` with `-t` because we want to show the TCP ports. As we only need to see listening ports, we can replace `-a` with `-l`:

```
$ sudo netstat -ltnp
```

We should see that the port we are trying to connect to is being held open by `rpc.mountd`. Of course, this is not allowed through the firewall.

 The port that `rpc.mountd` listens on may well be different to the port used on your system, so adjust the exercises to work with your `rpc.mountd` port and the port that is being used by your client.

The output from `tcpdump` is shown in the following screenshot. We can identify it as TCP traffic by additional properties, such as the sequence (`seq`) and window size (`win`), which we have highlighted in the following screenshot:

```
[vagrant@nfsclient ~]$ sudo tcpdump -nn -i enp0s8 host 192.168.10.10
tcpdump: verbose output suppressed, use -v or -vv for full protocol decode
listening on enp0s8, link-type EN10MB (Ethernet), capture size 65535 bytes
19:29:37.280163 IP 192.168.10.11.54733 > 192.168.10.10.111: UDP, length 56
19:29:37.281784 IP 192.168.10.10.111 > 192.168.10.11.54733: UDP, length 28
19:29:37.282503 IP 192.168.10.11.50632 > 192.168.10.10.20048: Flags [S], seq 1924098442, win 14600, o
ptions [mss 1460,sackOK,TS val 95811227 ecr 0,nop,wscale 6], length 0
19:29:37.282731 IP 192.168.10.10 > 192.168.10.11: ICMP host 192.168.10.10 unreachable - admin prohibi
ted, length 68
```

So now we can see that we also require the TCP port `20048` to be opened through the firewall on the NFS server; remember that the port may not be the same on your `nfshost`; we can remedy this very quickly using `firewall-cmd` from `nfshost` again as follows:

```
$ sudo firewall-cmd --add-port=20048/tcp --permanent
$ sudo firewall-cmd --reload
```

Now, we can return to the `nfsclient` as the `showmount` command should work correctly now, as shown in the following screenshot:

```
[vagrant@nfsclient ~]$ showmount -e 192.168.10.10
Export list for 192.168.10.10:
/var/exports/doc  *
/var/exports      192.168.10.11
[vagrant@nfsclient ~]$
```

Using static ports for NFSv3

The `portmapper` service is required for services that operate on non-static ports, which include the `rpc.mountd` and other NFSv3-based services. While configuring NFSv4 is simple because we only require access to the TCP port `2049` as the only requisite to the firewall, we still need access to more ports with v3 and most of these ports are non-static. Help is at hand though with the `/etc/sysconfig/nfs` file, where we can add entries enabling static ports for these services. The configuration is different on the RHEL 6 configuration. This is where search engines can often let you down with outdated documentations. This also includes the RHEL 7 documentation that is not up to date. Here, we show the correct settings that you will need in the `/etc/sysconfig/nfs` file to set static ports.

When you work on `nfshost` as root and use a text editor of your choice, you will need to edit the following lines:

```
RPCRQUOTADOPTS="-p 30001"
LOCKD_TCPPORT=30002
LOCKD_UDPPORT=30002
RPCMOUNTDOPTS="-p 30003"
STATDARG="-p 30004"
```

The ports used are nominal and you should choose ports that are not in use on your system. You can see that some services take the `-p` option to specify a port. The `rpc.lockd` utility has an actual port configuration. This was the RHEL 6 way of configuring all ports, but has changed on RHEL 7.

We will need to restart our services, and we can restart them individually or revisit the `for` loop that we used earlier. The edited loop is shown in the following code:

```
for s in rpcbind nfs-server nfs-lock nfs-idmap ; do
  sudo systemctl restart $s
done
```

We have now configured `nfshost` to use the static ports for these NFS services that will normally cause us an issue with dynamic ports. We still need the UDP port `111` configured in the firewall rules to allow access to `portmapper`, but we now know the ports that will be returned for other services and that they can be added. The final firewall configuration for NFSv3 using ports that we have configured are listed in the following command:

```
sudo firewall-cmd --add-port=111/udp --permanent
sudo firewall-cmd --add-port=2049/tcp --permanent
sudo firewall-cmd --add-port=30001/tcp --permanent
```

```
sudo firewall-cmd --add-port=30001/udp --permanent
sudo firewall-cmd --add-port=30002/tcp --permanent
sudo firewall-cmd --add-port=30002/udp --permanent
sudo firewall-cmd --add-port=30003/tcp --permanent
sudo firewall-cmd --add-port=30003/udp --permanent
sudo firewall-cmd --add-port=30004/tcp --permanent
sudo firewall-cmd --add-port=30004/udp --permanent
sudo firewall-cmd --reload
```

If we want to test the configuration fully with NFSv4, you will need to remove the crossmnt and fsid options from the exiting export definition because these are v4 options.

Configuring the NFS client

When mounting filesystems from a client, the default protocol implemented is NFSv4 on RHEL 7. We can explicitly set the protocol to v3 or v4, using the -t option to the mount command:

```
$ sudo mount -t nfs4 192.168.10.10:/var/exports /mnt   #NFS 4
$ sudo mount -t nfs 192.168.10.10:/var/exports /mnt     #NFS 3
```

In the following screenshot, you can see that we are able to connect from nfsclient using NFSv4 or NFSv3:

```
[vagrant@nfsclient ~]$
[vagrant@nfsclient ~]$
[vagrant@nfsclient ~]$ sudo mount -t nfs 192.168.10.10:/var/exports /mnt
[vagrant@nfsclient ~]$ sudo umount /mnt
[vagrant@nfsclient ~]$ sudo mount -t nfs4 192.168.10.10:/var/exports /mnt
[vagrant@nfsclient ~]$ sudo umount /mnt
[vagrant@nfsclient ~]$
```

Other mount options can be applied with the -o option to the mount command. You may consider the following command options:

* bg: This backgrounds the mount process
* rsize=xxxx: This specifies the maximum read size request in bytes
* wsize=xxxx: This specifies the maximum write buffer size in bytes

For more NFSv3 and NFSv4 mount options, these can be read in detail from the appropriate man page, as shown in the following command line:

```
$ man 5 nfs
```

Auto-mounting NFS with autofs

There is a client-side service called `autofs` that acts as an auto-mount service for both local and remote filesystems. This works with a kernel module and the user space service; as you enter a directory, the mount is created automatically. The `autofs` package needs to be installed along with the `nfs-utils` package if NFS mounts are to be made. The auto-mounting feature can work with other remote filesystems, not just NFS. To install `autofs`, use the following command:

```
$ sudo yum install -y autofs
```

With this installed, the default behavior is to use the `/net` directory point for the network hosts. We can then access shares or exports on any host that we have access to, and enter a directory that matches the server name or IP address after the `/net` directory. We only need to create top level directories and do not need to create subdirectories. We can just change the directories to `/net/192.168.10.10` and this directory will be created. Listing the contents of the directory will list the root level of the exports on the `nfshost`. This may sound too good to be true, so let's see this in action. First, we will create the directory and then start the service and enable it, as shown in the following command:

```
$ sudo mkdir /net
$ sudo systemctl start autofs
$ sudo systemctl enable autofs
```

With this in place, we can simply list the contents of the `/net/192.168.10.10` directory. We should see the top level of the export configuration. For us, this is currently the `/var` directory and the export directory is `/var/export`. If we have more top level directories exported, they too will show. The `/net/192.168.10.10` directory is created automatically and the default timeout for `autofs` is 300 seconds or 5 minutes. After 5 minutes of inactivity, a filesystem that is mounted will be automatically unmounted and the directory will disappear until it's needed again. This is a typical safe value; however, a specific timeout can be configured. We will see this later.

The following screenshot shows the four commands executed in order and the listing of the the temporary automount directory:

```
[vagrant@nfsclient ~]$
[vagrant@nfsclient ~]$ sudo mkdir /net
[vagrant@nfsclient ~]$ sudo systemctl start autofs
[vagrant@nfsclient ~]$ sudo systemctl enable autofs
ln -s '/usr/lib/systemd/system/autofs.service' '/etc/systemd/system/multi-user.target.wants/autofs.service'
[vagrant@nfsclient ~]$ ls /net/192.168.10.10
var
[vagrant@nfsclient ~]$ _
```

Auto-mounting directories on the client as they are required reduces the overhead on both the client and server, which is a really effective way of generating mounts. To define our own mounts points, we can edit the /etc/auto.master configuration file. We will add a top level directory as before.

In /etc/auto.master file, we will add the following command:

```
/corp /etc/auto.corp --timeout=600
```

This setting in the auto.master file tells the autofs service that when entering the /corp directory, the configuration can be read from the /etc/auto.corp file. Additionally, we have doubled the default timeout to 10 minutes for this auto-mount. We will need to create the top-level directory as follows:

```
$ sudo mkdir /corp
```

The configuration file for this directory should look similar to this in our case:

```
redhat -fstype=nfs4,rsize=4096,wsize=4096 192.168.10.10:/var/exports
```

With this entry, we will be able to see the contents of the server export while entering the /corp/redhat directory. We do not create the redhat subdirectory. Before testing, you will need to restart the autofs service:

```
$ sudo systemctl restart autofs
```

Now, we can access the /corp directory and it will be empty. This is shown in the following screenshot:

```
[vagrant@nfsclient ~]$ cd /corp
[vagrant@nfsclient corp]$ ls
[vagrant@nfsclient corp]$ _
```

If we now access the `redhat` directory, this does not show yet; we will be able to list the contents of the server's export. This is shown in the following screenshot:

```
[vagrant@nfsclient corp]$ cd redhat
[vagrant@nfsclient redhat]$ ls
doc   marketing
[vagrant@nfsclient redhat]$ _
```

I have been using this for years; it's still one of the most magical experiences on Linux.

Summary

I hope that you have found this chapter both intense and useful. There has been a lot of content to cover that has been made complicated by the need to cover both NFSv4 and NFSv3. Similar to most technologies, legacy clients need to be supported for some time. The great advantage this gave us was diagnosing firewall issues and using `tcpdump` in anger.

The main point with NFS and firewalling is to use NFSv4 wherever possible because we then only need to open the one static port: the TCP port 2049. For NFSv3, we need to assign static ports and often need to open both UDP and TCP ports to each protocol, depending on the client that connects.

Finishing the chapter on `autofs` is a real high note because this is so simple and effective to use, auto-creating directories and mounting them as required. What more could we wish for!

In the next chapter, we will stay with file sharing, but investigate sharing to Windows systems using Samba 4.

7
Implementing Windows Shares with Samba 4

Almost certainly, your Linux devices will not be running autonomously, and other operating systems will co-exist with them. No matter where your infrastructure is located, the likelihood is that you will need to interoperate with Windows systems at the very least. This is true just as much in the home environment as it's in the enterprise. Considering the home market, how many people do you know that use Windows desktops and have a Linux server as a central file store. Remember that the Linux server may be embedded into **Network Attached Storage (NAS)**, a device that you bought from the high street. Within enterprises, large and small, Microsoft's Active Directory is a very prevalent identity store that shares user accounts across a range of systems.

To help integrate RHEL 7 into your Windows environment, we will use this chapter to provide you with the basics on the following topics:

- Overview of Samba and Samba services
- Overview of the lab environment
- Configuring time and DNS
- Managing Samba services
- Samba client on RHEL 7
- Configuring file shares on Samba
- Troubleshooting Samba

An overview of Samba and Samba services

When investigating our main services and using Samba, we will need to install the `samba` package; this package can be installed as follows:

```
$ sudo yum install -y samba
```

With the package installed, the following services are added to our system:

- For file and print sharing, we have the `smbd` service. For this service, we will need to open TCP ports `139` and `445`.

- If we need to respond to legacy NetBIOS names requests, we will need to start the `nmbd` service. We will need this for older clients, such as Windows 95, 98, and ME. Windows 2000 and XP clients can make use of this network browsing protocol as well. Should we need this service, which somehow I doubt, we will need to open the UDP port `137`.

If you want to join a Windows domain, then you can add client tools packages such as `samba-winbind` or `sssd-common`.

If you use the `firewall-cmd` command, adding the Samba service will enable three ports for you. To add the Samba service to a firewall, we will use the following commands:

```
$ sudo firewall-cmd --permanent --add-service=samba
$ sudo firewall-cmd --reload
$ sudo firewall-cmd --list-services
```

The last command is for information purposes only and is not required to set the firewall rule.

An overview of the lab environment

For demonstrations is this chapter, we will use two virtual machines running in an **Oracle VirtualBox** virtualization environment.

We have a Microsoft Server 2008R2 Active Directory Domain Controller with the `192.168.0.252` IP address and the RHEL 7.1 host with the `192.168.0.69` IP address.

Configuring time and DNS

Although if we are using the RHEL host for a simple file and print sharing purpose, then obtaining an accurate time and DNS are not too much of an issue; however, we are most likely going to need to bring the RHEL server to an Active Directory domain so that we can make use of single sign-on. Users will be able to access their shares using the same credentials as they use in the Active Directory, rather than having a user account and password on the RHEL server.

In this chapter, we will just look at file sharing, and in *Chapter 8, Integrating RHEL 7 into Microsoft Active Directory Domains*, we bring the server to the AD domain.

In *Chapter 3, Configuring Key Network Services*, we configured time services. Now, let's look at how to set our `chronyd` time source to the Active Directory time server. If we are using NTP, then set the NTP time source to the Active Directory server. Alternatively, ensure that the Active Directory time source is set to the same time source that you use for your RHEL host.

To configure the time source on the Windows 2008R2 Active Directory Server, you will need to open an administrative Command Prompt and type the following commands:

```
c:\> net stop w32time
c:\> w32tm /config /syncfromflags:manual /manualpeerlist:"uk.pool.ntp.org"
c:\> w32tm /config /reliable:yes
c:\> net start w32time
c:\> w32tm /config /update
c:\> w32tm /resync
c:\> w32tm /query /status
```

The output from the final status subcommand is shown in the following screenshot:

```
C:\Users\Administrator>w32tm /query /status
Leap Indicator: 0(no warning)
Stratum: 4 (secondary reference - syncd by (S)NTP)
Precision: -6 (15.625ms per tick)
Root Delay: 0.0480499s
Root Dispersion: 7.8142363s
ReferenceId: 0x557750E8 (source IP:  85.119.80.232)
Last Successful Sync Time: 06/03/2015 08:34:51
Source: uk.pool.ntp.org
Poll Interval: 6 (64s)
```

I feel having accurate time on the network is a must, no matter you intend joining a domain or not.

To join the Active Directory domain, we must be able to resolve the service records that locate domain controllers. The easiest way to achieve this is to point the DNS resolvers of RHEL to the Active Directory Servers that host the DNS. I have just one domain controller and this is a DNS server as well. To ensure that we resolve these names correctly, we write to configuration files for interfaces on RHEL 7. On my system, these are as follows:

```
/etc/sysconfig/network-scripts/ifcfg-eno1677736
```

```
/etc/sysconfig/network-scripts/ifcfg-eno33554992
```

Ensure that the DNS1 entry point to the Active Directory domain controller and `PEERDNS=yes` is set in both files. Alternatively, configure the `/etc/resolv.conf` file with the settings of a name server and ensure that the `PEERDNS=no` attribute is set in all the interface files.

The following screenshot shows the first configuration option with the setting made in the interface file only:

```
TYPE="Ethernet"
BOOTPROTO="none"
DEVICE="eno16777736"
ONBOOT="yes"
DNS1=192.168.0.252
PEERDNS=yes
```

With this set in both interface files, (if you have two NICSNICs), you can simply restart the `NetworkManager` service as follows:

```
$ sudo systemctl restart NetworkManager
```

To test the configuration, you can try to resolve the name servers for your Active Directory domain hosted in DNS. For the book, we simply use example.com. To resolve this domain from the RHEL 7 host, we run the following command:

```
$ dig -t ns example.com
```

The `dig` command looks for records of the `ns` type or name servers from the `example.com` domain. The output should be similar to the following screenshot:

```
;; ANSWER SECTION:
example.com.                 3600    IN     NS      win-oafhmlnhii2.example.com.

;; ADDITIONAL SECTION:
win-oafhmlnhii2.example.com. 3600 IN     A       192.168.0.252
```

Managing Samba services

To access the resources of Samba, a user needs a POSIX (Linux) user account available to them and a Samba account. The POSIX account can be an ordinary account within the `/etc/passwd` file or this account can be centralized in LDAP or an Active Directory. When a POSIX account is enabled for Samba, additional attributes that are required by Windows systems are added to the user account. To enable an existing POSIX account with Samba, we can use the `/bin/pdbedit` command. This can work with Samba accounts in the following account stores:

- The `/etc/samba/smbpasswd` file
- The `tdbsam` database located at `/var/lib/samba/private/passdb.tdb` (this is the default samba account store)
- The OpenLDAP directory services

As existing domain accounts have the required attributes for Samba, there is no requirement to enable those accounts for Samba.

Firstly, we will list all existing Samba enabled accounts. Of course, we have only installed Samba and not enabled any other account. Also, we only have local accounts in the `/etc/passwd` file because the RHEL server is currently not part of a domain or LDAP:

```
$ sudo pdbedit -L
```

There should be no output to this command because we don't have any Samba enabled accounts. If you run a command as a standard user without errors, you will see permission violations while trying to access a database.

We will now enable the exiting account for `root` and the standard user: `andrew`. We will not only create an account and enable it for Samba, but also add attributes that are stored in the assigned Samba account's backend. In the default case, this is the `tdbsam` database. To enable these two accounts, use the following commands:

```
$ sudo pdbedit -a -u root
$ sudo pdbedit -a -u andrew
```

You will be prompted for a new Samba password for each account. Ideally, this should be different to their POSIX password. The truncated output after enabling the Samba account for `andrew` is shown in the following command line screenshot:

```
[andrew@redhat7 Desktop]$ sudo pdbedit -a -u andrew
new password:
retype new password:
Unix username:          andrew
NT username:
Account Flags:          [U          ]
User SID:               S-1-5-21-2762278993-3349253350-608103729-1001
Primary Group SID:      S-1-5-21-2762278993-3349253350-608103729-513
Full Name:              andrew
Home Directory:         \\redhat7\andrew
HomeDir Drive:
Logon Script:
Profile Path:           \\redhat7\andrew\profile
Domain:                 REDHAT7
```

Magically, when we run the list of accounts, we will be able to see these two accounts:

```
$ sudo pdbedit -L
```

The output should be similar to the following screenshot, adjusting the account names to match your own:

```
[andrew@redhat7 Desktop]$ sudo pdbedit -L
root:0:root
andrew:1000:andrew
```

You can use the -L option with -v for a verbose output similar to the information you see when enabling an account.

The main configuration file for Samba is `/etc/samba/smb.conf`. This file is segmented into sections and each section (with the exception of [global]) defines some form of shared resources. Each section is denoted with the section name in square brackets `[]`. In addition to the `[global]` section, there are two other special sections. These sections are defined in the following list:

- `[global]`: Attributes set within the global section refer to the Samba server as a whole rather than a particular shared resource.

- `[homes]`: The presence of this section allows users to connect to their own home directory easily and on the fly without any additional administrative effort to share a user's home directory. This can work without the need for the username and account name to be the same as the home directory name. The user: `andrew` will connect to his home share on the server in a manner similar to the following command:

    ```
    //<server-name or IP>/andrew
    ```

    The home directory attribute from the user account will be read and then the user will be connected to their assigned home directory.

- `[printers]`: The presence of this section allows local printers to be shared automatically with no further administrative effort. A user will use the following URL to connect to a printer:

    ```
    //<server-name or IP>/<printer-name>
    ```

You will find the `/etc/samba/smb.conf` file heavily commented with some comments with the # symbol and others with the semicolon (;) symbol. Both are valid comments, but its inconsistency is a little annoying.

If you would like to create a backup and remove empty and commented lines, try to run the following command from the `/etc/samba` directory:

```
$ sudo sed -i.bak '/^\s*[;#]/d;/^$/d;' smb.conf
```

The regular expression that we use to search for lines to delete is a little more complex than normal, but it still does an amazing job for us. There are two expressions for `sed` in the example, `/^\s*[;#]/d`.

The preceding expression will delete commented lines from the file.

We look for lines with (^) and any whitespace character (\s). Additionally, using *, we check for zero or more whitespace characters. In this way, we are allowing an optional whitespace character at the start of the line, but it must be followed by ; or # ([;#]) symbol. In simple English, this expands to lines that are commented, regardless of whether they start with a space/tab character or directly with a comment. The search string is delimited between the two / characters, and the d command is used to delete matching lines that follow:

```
/^$/d
```

The preceding expression deletes blank or empty lines from a file.

The effect that this has is that it reduces the line count of the file from 320 lines to 20 lines in seconds. We keep the original file as a backup, that is, smb.conf.bak.

A simple [global] section may look similar to the following screenshot:

```
[global]
        workgroup = MYGROUP
        server string = Samba Server Version %v
        log file = /var/log/samba/log.%m
        max log size = 50
        idmap config * : backend = tdb
        cups options = raw
```

These settings are detailed as follows:

* workgroup = MYGROUP: This denotes the NetBIOS workgroup to join in the Network Neighborhood view.
* server string = Samba Server Version %v: This appears as a description next to the server name within a network view. The %v variable will display the Samba version; in our case, this is 4.1.2.
* log file = /var/log/samba/log.%m: This specifies the path to the log file; the %m variable is the machine name (hostname).
* max log size = 50: This specifies the maximum size in KB for the log file before it is rotated.
* idmap config * : backend = tdb: This is the mapping mechanism to map POSIX user IDs and group ID to **SIDs (Security Identifiers)**.
* cups options = raw: These are the printer settings that tell the cupsCUPS process to send the job directly to the printer rather than trying to interpret it. It will have already been processed by a Windows printer driver and needs no further processing.

You can also use directives to control which hosts or networks can access the system with `hosts allow` and `hosts deny` directives. For example, the following attribute settings within the [global] section will only allow access to any share to the given network. The `127.0.0.1` host will always have access unless explicitly denied. Either of the following methods are correct, allowing access to `192.168.0.0/24`:

```
hosts allow = 192.168.0.
```

OR:

```
hosts allow = 192.168.0.0/255.255.255.0
```

These `host allow` settings and their sibling `host deny` settings can also be managed at the share level, but [global] settings will take precedence over anything configured at the share level.

If changes are made to a running configuration, then we can run a preflight check to test the integrity of our changes before restarting the service. To do this, we use the `testparm` command. We run this simply as root, as shown in the following command:

```
$ sudo testparm
```

The `nmb` and `smb` services are managed independently. We can start and enable the Samba file server with the following commands:

```
$ sudo systemctl enable smb
$ sudo systemctl start smb
```

As the [homes] section is configured by default, we are now ready to test the system.

The Samba client on RHEL 7

Currently, my firewall service is disabled, so I do not need to be concerned with the firewall; however, I will only need to add in the TCP port 445 and 139 or the `samba` service.

If we install the Samba client package, we can list all the shares available to a given user. This is shown in the following command extract:

```
$ sudo yum install -y samba-client
$ smbclient -U andrew -L //localhost
```

Once the Samba client is installed, we can use it to log in as andrew; we will be prompted for the password and to list shares on the localhost. We should see the listed home directory coming from the [homes] special share section. This is always there by default. We will see the output as expected, not the share name andrew, as shown in the following screenshot:

```
[root@redhat7 samba]# smbclient -U andrew -L //localhost
Enter andrew's password:
Domain=[MYGROUP] OS=[Unix] Server=[Samba 4.1.12]

        Sharename       Type        Comment
        ---------       ----        -------
        IPC$            IPC         IPC Service (Samba Server Version 4.1.12)
        andrew          Disk        Home Directories
Domain=[MYGROUP] OS=[Unix] Server=[Samba 4.1.12]
```

Of course, we can leave it here and hide the fact that there are some SELinux traps with the current setup. We can connect to a share, but SELinux will prevent access to the users' home directories. While *Chapter 10, Securing the System with SELinux*, will look at SELinux in more detail, we can simply and securely gain access to shares by one simple Boolean change. Firstly, we will test the current configuration. SELinux is in the enforcing mode and the firewall is not running. To mount the Samba share, we can use the following command written as a single line:

```
$ sudo mount -t cifs -o username=andrew,password=Password1
//192.168.0.69/andrew /mnt
```

We do not need to include the password in mount options; if we don't, we will be prompted for the user's Samba password during the mount process. This should succeed, but if we try to access the mount target (in this case /mnt), we will be denied access. To overcome this, we can interrogate the SELinux configuration for Samba home directories. The following command illustrates how this is achieved:

```
$ getsebool samba_enable_home_dirs
```

In Samba, the default configuration settings are turned off and as such prevents access to the home directory. We enable the Samba service using the following command:

```
$ sudo setsebool -P samba_enable_home_dirs on
```

With Boolean enabled, we gain immediate access to a share. There is no requirement to unmount and remount the home directory. The -P option makes this change permanent so that we can be assured that the change persists until we need to disable the setting, and the system is still secured with SELinux.

To see a list of SELinux, Samba Booleans, and their settings, you can use the following command:

```
$ getsebool -a | grep samba
```

Of course, we can also connect to a share from a Windows device provided we have the correct credentials. The following screenshot shows the mapped drive from the Windows 2008R2 server connected to Andrew's home directory:

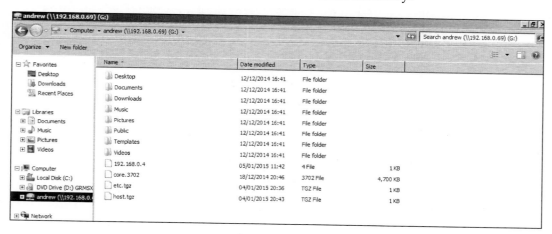

Configuring file shares in Samba

We have seen the major feature of file sharing that Samba enables with the user's home directories. Although this feature is enabled by default, we will also need to create our own file shares by adding our own sections to `smb.conf`. On the Red Hat server, we have the `/data` directory that we worked with during `btrfs` in *Chapter 5, Implementing btrfs*. If we need to share this to our Windows-based clients, then Samba is the tool we will use.

We can edit the `smb.conf` file with root privileges and add a new section to the configuration. The attributes that we use in the section control the access and use of the share. At the very least, we require the path attribute for the share to be meaningful. For a full list of options, the `man` pages for the `smb.conf` file will help. The following screenshot shows the share definition that we have added for the `/data` directory on the server:

```
[data]
path = /data
read only = yes
read list = andrew,root,@users
```

The read list restricts reading data from the share to listed users; in this case, we add a group. The @ symbol denotes a group within the list.

We still need to work with SELinux a little here by changing the SELinux context of the /data directory and its contents. We can achieve this with the chcon command for the changed context:

```
$ sudo chcon -R -t samba_share_t /data
```

Do not forget to test the configuration using testparm; if all is okay, we can restart the smb service as follows:

```
$ sudo systemctl restart smb
```

Now, we can browse and access the Samba shares that we have defined. Using the Windows 2008R2 server, we can now browse the network and see the home directory for andrew share and data share. The following screenshot shows this:

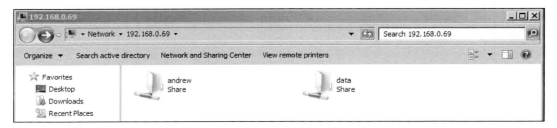

We can see why Samba is such an important tool in small and large environments; file sharing is just so simple and integrates into our existing infrastructure.

Troubleshooting Samba

If we are having problems with Samba, we can always check the output from the testparm command again and ensure that we have not missed anything vital. We can check which setting is valid from the man pages for smb.conf should be concerned over some settings.

We can also check the log files. These are located in the /var/log/samba/ directory.

There will be logs that represent client access, as shown in the following command:

```
log.<client ip-address>
```

OR:

```
log.<client-hostname>
```

There will also be the `log.smbd` daemon log.

If you need more details on the daemon log, set the log level attribute in the `[global]` section of the `smb.conf` as follows:

```
log level = 3
```

This raises the verbosity of logging, which may help. We suggest not leaving the level set this high and removing the setting when it's no longer required. The log level can be configured from 0 to 10, where 0 is low and 10 is high, but level 3 is as verbose as most people will need.

Summary

In this chapter, we looked at how to share filesystems with Windows clients without the need to disable SELinux. I do hope that you appreciate its importance and see the ease of leaving SELinux in place once we are aware of its basics.

Although we did not implement the firewall in this chapter, we did again review the `firewalld` settings to make this happen. Firewalling with `firewalld` is covered in *Chapter 11, Network Security with firewalld*.

In the next chapter, we will look at how to integrate RHEL 7 into a Windows Active Directory domain.

8
Integrating RHEL 7 into Microsoft Active Directory Domains

In the previous chapter, we looked at how to share resources to Microsoft's clients. Now, in the spirit of true symbiosis, we will see how RHEL can make use of Active Directory users and groups, implementing domains as identity stores. If users have access to the console of the RHEL server, then simply by their Active Directory credentials, they will have access to RHEL. Not only does this streamline access to a console, but it also simplifies access to any shared folder on the RHEL 7 Samba server.

We will structure this chapter so that you are able to see the bells and whistles (the good stuff) that Active Directory integration can provide before we delve under the hood at what goes on to make these simple tools work.

In this chapter, we will cover the following topics:

- Overview of identity management
- Overview of the lab environment
- Preparing to join an Active Directory domain
- Using realm to manage domain enrolment
- Logging on to RHEL 7 using Active Directory credentials
- User and group management with `adcli`
- Delegating Active Directory accounts with `sudo`
- Leaving a domain
- Understanding Active Directory as an identity provider for `sssd`

Overview of identity management

To begin our banquet of delights, we will focus on the importance of identity management in an enterprise. Without using some form of identity store or vault to centralize user accounts, these accounts will need to be duplicated because access is required for other systems. As you can imagine, these user accounts can quickly become out of control as vast numbers are created to support individual account silos on each system. However, we should not be too concerned with the need for creation and management of these accounts; other than this, being an administrative burden is not a security concern. If a user does not have access to a resource, they will soon let you know. The concern with account silos is what happens when a user leaves; do you believe that every account for every user that leaves an organization will be deleted or (at least) disabled. Somehow, however good your system, some will slip through the net and a security issue will be created. Good identity management with one account per user will solve the administrative burden, and more importantly, the security weakness.

Of course, lesser issues relate to the management of these accounts, such as password changes, and perhaps the need for name changes as time progresses. Ideally, each user in an organization will have just one identity, which is a single set of credentials that they use to gain access to any resource to which they have permission. This can be achieved through some form of central directory service acting as an identity vault. This may be the Active Directory, but it can quite easily be some other form of the **LDAP (Lightweight Directory Access Protocol)** server. In small to medium environments, an Active Directory may be sufficient, but as the organization grows and the size of the identity vault grows, perhaps the need for a completely separate directory for users will be needed. The central user store can then synchronize changes to other connected systems.

Microsoft has its Identity Management suite to build around the Active Directory, and Red Hat has its identity management directory server. This chapter will focus and integrate RHEL 7 directly into a single Domain Active Directory environment.

An overview of the lab environment

For demonstrations in this chapter, we will use two virtual machines running in an **Oracle VirtualBox** virtualization environment.

We have a Microsoft Server 2008R2 Active Directory Domain Controller with the IP address 192.168.0.252 and the RHEL 7.1 host with the IP address 192.168.0.69. This is the same setup that we have used in *Chapter 7, Implementing Windows Shares with Samba 4*; we have left time and DNS configured the same way. If you are stepping into this chapter without having completed *Chapter 7, Implementing Windows Shares with Samba 4*, ensure that you have set up the RHEL server to use the Domain Controller for both the time and name resolution.

Preparing to join an Active Directory domain

From what we have seen in *Chapter 7, Implementing Windows Shares with Samba 4*, using Samba to share files, we can understand that this is pretty impressive stuff. We always need to remind ourselves that this all comes without any price tag or the need of client access licenses.

>
> Samba file sharing is free, that is, *without cost* and free in *liberty*; you can use it as you wish. This is the fundamental premise of open source software and is at the heart of Linux.

The big issue that may act as a potential deal breaker is the need to maintain user accounts on the RHEL server and the AD domain to which the workstation accessing the server belongs. If we implement more than one server, the problem is exacerbated with the need for accounts on each and every server as well as the AD domain. The simple solution is to incorporate the RHEL server into the AD domain and use AD accounts for resource access. In this way, we can use a single sign-on to the Active Directory and gain access to shared resources on the RHEL Samba server.

>
> If the Active Directory is not in place, the central account sharing can be established by installing the openLDAP server on RHEL. One RHEL server can then act as an identity vault, sharing accounts to LDAP clients on other servers.

Irrespective of Samba file shares, your Active Directory users may need access to RHEL servers via SSH or some other mechanism. They will need accounts defined on each RHEL server for this. Joining an RHEL server to the AD domain enables the use of the user's AD account when logging in to any member server, which includes RHEL servers or desktops. Additionally, rights can be delegated to these accounts using the /etc/sudoers file and file permissions in the normal mechanism.

Before we join the AD domain, we need to ensure that we have set up the time services and DNS, as detailed in *Chapter 7, Implementing Windows Shares with Samba 4*. With these infrastructure services in place, we will need the following packages installed on the RHEL server:

- `realmd`: This manages enrolment and membership to the Active Directory domains
- `samba`: This denotes the Samba services
- `samba-common`: This denotes the shared tools for servers and clients
- `oddjob`: This is a D-bus service that runs the odd jobs for clients
- `oddjob-mkhomedir`: This is used with the odd job services to create home directories for AD accounts, if needed
- `sssd`: The System Security Services daemon can be used to divert client authentication as required
- `adcli`: These are the tools for joining and managing AD domains

The following command shows the installation of necessary packages:

```
$ sudo yum install oddjob realmd samba samba-common oddjob-mkhomedir sssd adcli
```

Using realm to manage domain enrolment

With these packages installed, we can use the `realm` command to manage our enrolments. This command is part of the `realmd` package that we added. We can use the list subcommand to ensure that we are not currently part of a domain:

```
$ realm list
```

The output should be blank. Now, we are ready to proceed with the next step: joining the domain. With a simple environment, you will know the domain that you want to join; at least we certainly hope that you do. In our case, we do know it and this is `example.com`. Using the discover subcommand, we can verify that we have all the required packages installed, as shown in the following command extract:

```
$ realm discover example.com
```

The output from this command will list that this is an Active Directory domain and the required packages that we should have in place before joining the AD domain. The following screenshot illustrates this:

```
[andrew@redhat7 Desktop]$ sudo realm discover example.com
example.com
  type: kerberos
  realm-name: EXAMPLE.COM
  domain-name: example.com
  configured: no
  server-software: active-directory
  client-software: sssd
  required-package: oddjob
  required-package: oddjob-mkhomedir
  required-package: sssd
  required-package: adcli
  required-package: samba-common
[andrew@redhat7 Desktop]$ 
```

Depending on your Active Directory functionality level, you may require either the `samba-windbind` or `sssd` packages. We are using Active Directory on 2008R2 with the default level of Windows Server 2003 configured. At this stage, you should verify that you have all the required packages installed.

> If we do not need to share resources we do not need the `samba` package; `samba` is only used to share, not to join domains.

As this is a Kerberos domain type, the `join` subcommand will join the server to the domain as a member server and initialize the `/etc/krb5.keytab` Kerberos keytab file and the `/etc/krb5.conf` configuration file. There will be more detail on these files that act behind the scenes given at the end of the chapter. To join the AD domain, add the computer to the default folder in the AD domain using the following command:

```
$ sudo realm join --user=administrator@example.com example.com
```

Should you want to add it to a designated Organizational Unit within the Active Directory, you will first need to create the OU, or at least ensure that it exists. With the OU being present, the command will be similar to the following, where we add to the Linux OU:

```
$ sudo realm join --computer-ou="OU=Linux" \ --user=administrator@
example.com example.com
```

This is the method we will use to add the RHEL server to a path:

`OU=Linux,DC=example,DC=com`

With either of these methods, you will be prompted for the domain administrator's password or the password of a user with delegated rights to add computers to the AD domain and your `sudo` user's password (if required). The command can take a few minutes to take effect, so give it time until the shell prompt is returned. As a standard user, you can then list the domain you have joined using the `realm list` command again. We should note that the output at first may seem similar to the `realm discover example.com` command that we ran earlier; however, on closer examination, we will see that we are now a member server, as shown by `configured: kerberos-member` in the following command:

`$ realm list`

The output from the preceding command is shown in the following screenshot:

```
[andrew@redhat7 Desktop]$ realm list
example.com
  type: kerberos
  realm-name: EXAMPLE.COM
  domain-name: example.com
  configured: kerberos-member
  server-software: active-directory
  client-software: sssd
  required-package: oddjob
  required-package: oddjob-mkhomedir
  required-package: sssd
  required-package: adcli
  required-package: samba-common
  login-formats: %U@example.com
  login-policy: allow-realm-logins
[andrew@redhat7 Desktop]$
```

Logging on to RHEL 7 using Active Directory credentials

Welcome to the world of centralized accounts. I think you will have to concede that the process was very simple using RHEL 7 and vastly more simple than the previous releases of RHEL. We are now ready to make use of central user accounts from the Active Directory.

To log on to the RHEL 7 server, we can use the Active Directory **UPN (User Principal Name)**. This is in the format of `user@<Fully Qualified Domain Name>`. For example, if we have an account in the `example.com` domain named `jjones`, we can log on to the RHEL server using the following command:

`jjones@example.com`

The following screenshot shows this process as we use the `switch user` command to log on as the AD account for `jjones`. Note that as the home directory for `jjones` does not exist, `oddjob` kindly creates it for us, as shown in the following screenshot:

```
[andrew@redhat7 Desktop]$ su - jjones@example.com
Password:
Creating home directory for jjones@example.com.
[jjones@example.com@redhat7 ~]$ ▮
```

To connect remotely using SSH tools, such as PuTTY for Windows, we will use the following syntax implementing two @ symbols; this may look a little weird, but is correct:

`jjones@example.com@192.168.0.69`

An SSH connection to RHEL from the Windows PuTTY client is shown in the following screenshot:

```
jjones@example.com@192.168.0.69's password:
Last login: Sat Mar  7 19:18:47 2015
[jjones@example.com@redhat7 ~]$ _
```

We have now seen that we can make use of Active Directory accounts on our Linux systems. With the Red Hat server as part of our domain, we can log on to Linux with a single set of credentials. When a user leaves an organization, there is now only a solitary user account to delete or disable. We have seen this in action on a single server, but this equally applies to all your RHEL 7 or CentOS 7 servers and desktops; this process is the same across the board, making us efficient and secure.

User and group management with adcli

We are not just restricted to consuming these domain accounts; we also have a level of management of Active Directory from the command line of our Linux servers. With the correct privileges in Active Directory, we can:

- Create users and groups
- Modify group memberships
- Delete users and groups

Although the tools are not as rich as you will find with the native OS, especially when using PowerShell, there is a need and advantage to some of the management provided by Linux devices.

If you are a Linux administrator and work mainly on Linux, it does make sense for you to add Active Directory users to groups that you use for delegation on Linux. For example, you can maintain an Active Directory group called `LinuxAdmins` and delegate rights via the `/etc/sudoers` file to this group. It's quite correct that you maintain and control the AD group and not necessarily the `Domain Admins` group in the AD.

Listing the Active Directory information

To begin with the `adcli` command, we will take a look at the `info` subcommand. This can display details on domains and the domain controllers that are discovered. We can run this command as a standard user, as shown in the following command:

```
$ adcli info example.com
```

The output will show the Active Directory roles for the domain controller and details on the site, as shown in the following screenshot:

```
[andrew@redhat7 ~]$ adcli info example.com
[domain]
domain-name = example.com
domain-short = EXAMPLE
domain-forest = example.com
domain-controller = WIN-OAFHMLNHII2.example.com
domain-controller-site = Default-First-Site-Name
domain-controller-flags = pdc gc ldap ds kdc timeserv closest writable full-secr
et ads-web
domain-controller-usable = yes
domain-controllers = WIN-OAFHMLNHII2.example.com
[computer]
computer-site = Default-First-Site-Name
[andrew@redhat7 ~]$ 
```

In this way, we will be able to verify the connection and the domain controller that we are connected to.

Creating Active Directory users

This command is probably not one of the most useful tools given that we can create the user, but can't enable the account or set the password for the new user. In this way, the command is less useful than some of the other tools with `adcli`. A sample command is as follows:

```
$ adcli create-user fjones --domain=example.com --display-name="Fred
Jones"
```

This command will try to log on to a domain as an administrator and will prompt for the password. To log on as a different user, you may make use of the `-U` or `--login-user` option.

For completeness, we cover the `create user` command, but in reality, the user will still need to be enabled and have the password set in the Active Directory.

To delete the account we just created, we will use the following command:

```
$ adcli delete-user   --domain=example.com fjones
```

Creating Active Directory groups

In many respects, the `adcli` command is very useful to us as Linux administrators. So, as long as our domain accounts have rights to create and manage groups in the AD, it's correct that we should be the ones managing the group membership that affect the Linux access. Assuming that the user accounts are already created, we do not need to concern ourselves with password management on the creation and membership of these groups. We will use the administrator account while accessing the domain as before, but we could use our own account if it had the privileges.

To create the Linux users group in the Linux OU where we have placed the server, we will use the following command:

```
$ adcli create-group --domain=example.com \ --domain-
ou="OU=Linux,DC=example,dc=com" "Linux Users"
```

We can verify that this has worked as expected by navigating to the **OU** (**Organizational Unit**) within the Active Directory users and computers on the domain controller. In the following screenshot, we can see that we have the server group and the new group:

We will keep the created group as it is, because we will add users to it; the process of deleting a group is similar to the process of deleting a user, as shown in the following command:

```
$ adcli delete-group  --domain=example.com "Linux Users"
```

Should we need help on any command, we can issue syntax help with commands similar to the following command:

```
$ adcli delete-group --help
```

Just use the correct subcommand that you need help with.

Managing the Active Directory group membership

Now that we have the Linux users group, we can manage the membership of this group. Within the AD domain, we have the `jjones` user that we can add to this group. The following command shows how this is done using our domain:

```
$ adcli add-member  --domain=example.com "Linux Users" jjones
```

> Other than when you create a group or user in a given context, we can refer to the object by the SAMAccountName attribute alone (the user or group name). This is a unique identifier in a domain. In the preceding example, we can simply refer to the group as Linux Users and the user as jjones. Quotes are required to protect the space used in the group name.

Delegating Active Directory accounts with sudo

Being able to manage the Active Directory group membership is fundamental to our management of Linux. We can assign the ownership of files and directories to these groups and (more importantly) the delegate rights on the system using the `/etc/sudoers` file.

Let's see how this delegation works. We will create a new group in the Active Directory and add an administrator to this group. As a simple setup, we are limited to users that we have created, as shown in the following commands:

```
$ adcli create-group  --domain=example.com \ --domain-
ou="OU=Linux,DC=example,dc=com" "Linux Admins"

$ adcli add-member  --domain=example.com "Linux Admins" Administrator
```

We now have two groups that we may want to use for delegation: `Linux Users` and `Linux Admins`. To delegate with the `sudoers` system, we run the `visudo` command as a root user or with `sudo`. This file can be used as delegation, which allows selected commands to be run as root by selected users. These commands have to be prefaced with the `sudo` command. You can think of `sudo` as a similar command to `runas` in a Windows system:

```
$ sudo visudo
```

This will open the `/etc/sudoers` file for editing purposes. We can use G to move towards the end of the file and then o to insert a new line.

We will add these two lines of code to the `/etc/sudoers` file:

```
%Linux\ Admins@example.com ALL=(root) ALL %Linux\ Users@example.com
ALL=(root) /sbin/mount /mnt/cdrom, /sbin/umount /mnt/cdrom
```

 Note the use of \ to protect the space here. This is required because the `sudoers` file does not like the use of quotes.

The Linux admins group is allowed to run all commands on the system as root using `sudo`. The Linux users group can run the `mount` and `umount` commands only to mount and unmount the `cdrom` device.

With all the changes made in `vi`, we can use the ESC key to exit and `:x` to save and exit the insert mode.

The following screenshot from the example system shows the changes as they should appear:

```
%Linux\ Admins@example.com ALL=(root) ALL
%Linux\ Users@example.com ALL=(root) /sbin/mount /mnt/cdrom, /sbin/umount /mnt/cdrom
```

When we log on as `jjones`, We will now find that we have the membership of the `Linux Users` group and `Linux Admins` for the `Administrator`. Additionally, both users will belong to the `Domain Users` group.

We can run the following command as a user of either group:

`$ id -Gn`

The preceding command will display the group names that the user belongs to. The domain administrator account will have several group memberships, but it will importantly include the `Linux Admins` group. This will allow users to run all commands prefixed with `sudo` so that they can run as root, as we have seen with the `andrew` account that had similar rights delegated.

The following screenshot shows the output of the `id` command when it is run as the administrator:

```
[administrator@example.com@redhat7 ~]$ id -Gn
domain users@example.com domain admins@example.com schema admins@example.com ent
erprise admins@example.com group policy creator owners@example.com denied rodc p
assword replication group@example.com linux admins@example.com
[administrator@example.com@redhat7 ~]$
```

We can also assign the filesystem ownership to users and groups from the directories. While we are still logged in to the RHEL 7.1 system as the domain administrator account, we will prove that the `sudo` entry is correct by changing the group ownership of a directory; this is something normally reserved for root:

`$ sudo chgrp Linux\ Usersexample.com /data`

`$ ls -ld /data`

In the preceding example, we changed the group ownership of the /data directory to the Linux Users group; subsequently, we displayed the ownership of the directory as well. For additional clarity, we have included a screenshot to demonstrate this process:

```
[administrator@example.com@redhat7 ~]$
[administrator@example.com@redhat7 ~]$ sudo chgrp Linux\ Users@example.com /data
[administrator@example.com@redhat7 ~]$ ls -ld /data
drwxr-xr-x. 4 root linux users@example.com 32 Feb 19 12:45 /data
[administrator@example.com@redhat7 ~]$
```

Leaving a domain

Until now, we have been able to demonstrate true interoperability with the Active Directory through the use of delegated permissions using sudo and ownership of files and directories with filesystems. This is outstanding and nothing less than what you would expect from an Enterprise Linux system; however outstanding this may be, there will be occurrences where the Linux server needs to be removed from a domain. Often, this is the case where it is removed from one domain before being added to another. Should this be required, the realm command makes the process easy, reversing the operation to the join subcommand as follows:

```
$ sudo realm leave example.com --remove
```

The additional option: --remove will ensure that the computer account is also deleted from the domain; otherwise, it should be deleted separately. For the moment, we will leave the computer in the domain.

Understanding Active Directory as an identity provider for sssd

In many ways, something this simple is very welcome on Linux; however, the simplicity is in masking the complex series of events and procedures that occur behind the scenes. It's now time to delve into what makes sssd work.

We first need to remind ourselves of all the configurations that we added in the only manual part of the process, that is, setting up the infrastructure services of time and DNS required for integration into the Active Directory. The following diagram shows the relationship between the RHEL server and Active Directory:

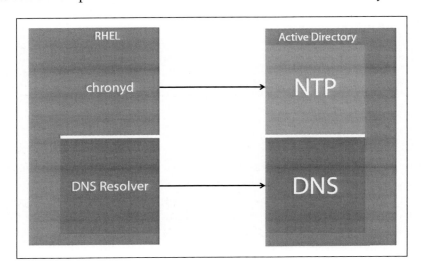

When we interrogated the Active Directory domain with `realm`, we could see from the resulting information that we required the `sssd` package among others. The System Security Services Daemon (`sssd`) provides a set of daemons to manage access to remote directories and authenticate mechanisms, in our case, the Active Directory. The `sssd` service provides the **NSS (Name Service Switch)** and **PAM (Pluggable Authentication Mechanism)** interface for our system and a modular backend system to connect to multiple different account sources and the D-bus interface as well. With this in mind, we should understand that both NSS and PAM modules have been added and configured for us on the system.

Identifying accounts on the remote Active Directory is performed over LDAP and authentication is done via Kerberos to the AD domain. The LDAP account search is referenced and calls for the `/usr/lib64/libnss_sss.so.2` NSS module and the `/etc/nsswitch.conf` file. Authentication will be referenced using `/lib64/security/pam_nss.so`.

We can expand the relationship diagram to include sssd as follows:

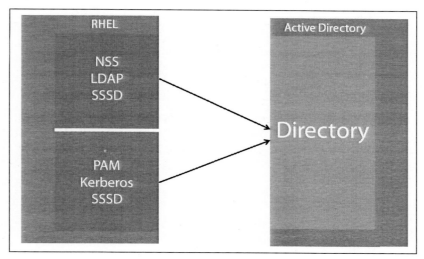

Configuring NSS

The **Name Service Switch (NSS)** configuration file, /etc/nsswitch.conf, is used by various NSS libraries; one of the NSS libraries is /usr/lib64/libnss_sss.so.2. The NSS configuration file determines the sources from which you can obtain the name service information and its order from a range of categories. Each category of information is identified by a resource database name; this can be hosts for name resolution and passwd for a database to locate user accounts.

In my opinion, the simplest approach is to use the hosts database to explain how these forces work. The entry in the /etc/nsswitch.conf for hosts is as follows:

```
hosts:      files dns
```

With the settings in effect, the preceding name resolution is achieved by first resolving names from the /etc/hosts local file and then via DNS resolver libraries. If you reversed these entries, the DNS will be checked before the local file.

If we check for sss within a file, we can see all the databases that rely on a particular library. The grep command can be used to isolate these entries, as shown in the following command:

```
$ grep sss /etc/nsswitch.conf
```

The result of the query should look similar to the following screenshot:

```
passwd:      files sss
shadow:      files sss
group:       files sss
services:    files sss
netgroup:    files sss
automount:   files sss
```

These are default settings, but we are not forced to accept them; we can implement changes if required. However, this order is probably the best as it allows local accounts to be resolved before searching for a domain (not that domain accounts will clash because they are specified with the full UPN of the user.

The database names are explained here:

- `passwd`: This specifies the user accounts
- `shadow`: This denotes the password information
- `group`: This specifies the group accounts
- `services`: This denotes the service name resolution
- `netgroup`: This specifies the groups of hosts that can be used in access control rules
- `automount`: This denotes the directories to be auto-mounted by `autofs`

In many setups, it's easy to disable the bottom three elements: `services`, `netgroup`, and `automount`. This will help tune the directory access, for example, if you leave the default settings when you run tools, such as `netstat`, to query which ports are open on the server, you will also run an LDAP query in the AD to resolve port addresses to service names with the service database entry in the `/etc/nsswitch.conf`.

The entry for the services will read similar to the following command to prevent LDAP lookups:

```
services: files
```

Configuring PAM

We can often leave **Pluggable Authentication Modules (PAM)** as they are, but we will look at their configuration here.

The services that can use PAM are configured with the associated PAM modules that they should use within a file in the `/etc/pam.d` directory. The can be in individual files, such as `/etc/pam.d/login`, or through command files that are referenced by many services (such as `/etc/pam.d/system-auth-ac`).

We can display the configuration that `sssd` uses with PAM using `grep` again to filter `sss` from the `/etc/pam.d/system-auth-ac` file. The output is shown in the following screenshot:

```
[root@redhat7 pam.d]# grep sss system-auth-ac
auth         sufficient    pam_sss.so use_first_pass
account      [default=bad success=ok user_unknown=ignore] pam_sss.so
password     sufficient    pam_sss.so use_authtok
session      optional      pam_sss.so
```

We can see that the authentication module is used for all possible triggers:

- `auth`: This is used during authentication
- `account`: This is used for account restrictions
- `password`: This is used for password change events
- `session`: This is used during a logged in session

Let's see some arguments (such as `use_first_pass`) that are used with the authentication module. Some of the possible arguments are stated as follows:

- `forward_pass`: The entered password can be used for other modules
- `use_first_pass`: Does not prompt for a password, but uses a previously entered password
- `use_authtok`: When changing a password, the previously entered password can be used to authenticate the password change
- `retry=N`: If this is set, the user can be prompted more than once for the password if they enter the wrong password

Configuring Kerberos

When you join a domain using realm, the `/etc/krb5.conf` keytab file is created to authenticate the RHEL system to the domain alongside the `/etc/krb5.conf` file. Having tidied the file, after removing comments for our domain, the file looks similar to the following screenshot:

```
[logging]
 default = FILE:/var/log/krb5libs.log
 kdc = FILE:/var/log/krb5kdc.log
 admin_server = FILE:/var/log/kadmind.log
[libdefaults]
 dns_lookup_realm = false
 ticket_lifetime = 24h
 renew_lifetime = 7d
 forwardable = true
 rdns = false
 default_ccache_name = KEYRING:persistent:%{uid}
 default_realm = EXAMPLE.COM
[realms]
 EXAMPLE.COM = {
 }
[domain_realm]
 example.com = EXAMPLE.COM
 .example.com = EXAMPLE.COM
```

We can see that the `/etc/krb5.conf` file has four sections:

- `logging`
- `libdefaults`
- `realms`
- `domain_realm`

As the demonstration lab is very small with just a single domain controller, there is no need to make changes. If you have a larger setup, you may want to add some more details to the realm. You can point to the local domain controllers holding the correct roles; otherwise, just let the DNS service records resolve these records as follows:

```
[realms]
EXAMPLE.COM {
 kdc = ad1.example.com
 admin_server = ad1.example.com
}
```

Configuring SSSD

The configuration for sssd can be found in the /etc/sssd/sssd.conf file. We have seen that this works for us by default, but there is room for customization, as shown in the following screenshot:

```
[sssd]
domains = example.com
config_file_version = 2
services = nss, pam

[domain/example.com]
ad_domain = example.com
krb5_realm = EXAMPLE.COM
realmd_tags = manages-system joined-with-samba
cache_credentials = True
id_provider = ad
krb5_store_password_if_offline = True
default_shell = /bin/bash
ldap_id_mapping = True
use_fully_qualified_names = True
fallback_homedir = /home/%d/%u
access provider = ad
```

A simple change here will be to change the home directory location of the AD users. By default, this is /home/example.com/username. If you have added the Unix extensions to the Active Directory, then we will set ldap_id_mapping to false and the UID and GID will be set in the Active Directory.

Summary

In this chapter, we looked at how to use the Active Directory as an identity store, utilizing users and groups on Linux. The ease of setting this up makes this a very usable and much-needed solution within corporations throughout the world.

There is a little bit of ground work required before setting up the time and DNS. Once this is set, then configuring sssd to use Active Directory as an identity source with the command realm is really a doddle.

With the RHEL system in the AD domain, we can manage this domain to a degree with adcli and give users' access to the Linux command line through a console or via SSH.

Next up, we will be staying a little with file sharing, but this time, we will use the Apache HTTPD web server.

9
Deploying the Apache HTTPD Server

The **Hypertext Transfer Protocol (HTTP)** server will be commonly referred to as a web server. As the name suggests, this is a network service that provides content to a client, typically a web browser, on the Internet. This typically means delivery of web pages, but any other documents can be served, such as images, sound, video, and even ISO files for RHEL.

The web server packaged on RHEL 7 is the Apache httpd service. This is the most common web server found on the Internet and developed by the Apache Software Foundation. RHEL has updated httpd to version 2.4, replacing the 2.2 release that has been in use in previous editions of RHEL.

In this chapter we will cover the following topics:

- Configuring the httpd service
- Controlling the httpd service
- Adding server modules
- Using virtual hosts

Configuring the httpd service

The Apache httpd web server can serve pages to clients on the Internet or locally on our internal intranet, so don't feel that you will have to necessarily ramp up security if you are deploying a web server. Of course, if the website is to be facing the Internet, additional security and isolation of this service may be required. However, we are working in a lab environment and will focus more on the configuration of the web server.

Installing Apache 2.4

The required packages are unlikely to be installed by default, so we will need to at least add the `httpd` package. Additionally, you may like to add the documentation. Consider only adding the documentation to a development server; I would not recommend adding it to a production server. We will add both packages to a server as follows:

```
$ sudo yum install httpd httpd-manual
```

Even at this stage, with so little effort added, we can start our service and browser to the web server using the following commands:

```
$ sudo systemctl start httpd
$ sudo systemct enable httpd
```

If we have a graphic environment, we can use Firefox from our local system to browse the localhost. We will be rewarded with a welcome page similar to the following screenshot:

Although I would like to think that my work here is done; somehow, I feel that you may just want a little more guidance.

The configuration

The configuration base for the `httpd` service on RHEL 7 is the `/etc/httpd` directory. With the `tree` command, we can effectively illustrate the configuration hierarchy or service. The single configuration required here is `httpd.conf`, but Red Hat is taking a much more modular approach and now includes many sub-configurations to the main file. The following screenshot from the output of the tree shows all files in place after the default installation:

```
[root@redhat7 httpd]# tree .
.
|-- conf
|   |-- httpd.conf
|   `-- magic
|-- conf.d
|   |-- autoindex.conf
|   |-- manual.conf
|   |-- README
|   |-- userdir.conf
|   `-- welcome.conf
|-- conf.modules.d
|   |-- 00-base.conf
|   |-- 00-dav.conf
|   |-- 00-lua.conf
|   |-- 00-mpm.conf
|   |-- 00-proxy.conf
|   |-- 00-systemd.conf
|   `-- 01-cgi.conf
|-- logs -> ../../var/log/httpd
|-- modules -> ../../usr/lib64/httpd/modules
`-- run -> /run/httpd
```

 If the preceding tree is not installed, it can be installed using sudo yum install tree.

The tree command has been run from the /etc/httpd directory. We can see the /etc/httpd/conf/httpd.conf file, which is the main configuration file. This includes other files from /etc/httpd/conf.d and /etc/httpd/conf.modules.d. Also, there are three symbolically linked directories:

- logs
- modules
- run

The content of a page that we see when we browse through a site comes from the configuration in /etc/httpd/conf.d/welcome.conf. When no actual website content exists, the default welcome page is generated.

With the inclusion of the userdir.conf and autoindex.conf files, the separate modules configuration is very different from the httpd configuration on RHEL 6, where these were all part of the main httpd.conf file.

We have already mentioned that the configuration root of the web server is the `/etc/httpd` directory. The configuration for this is in the `/etc/httpd/conf/httpd.conf` file. Some of the key directives from this file are as follows:

- `ServerRoot: /etc/httpd`
- `DocumentRoot: /var/www/html`
- `DirectoryIndex: index.html`

The `ServerRoot` directive, as we have seen is where we can locate configurations, logs, and modules for the web server. The `DocumentRoot` directive represents where the web content can be found, whereas the `DirectoryIndex` HTML page is the default page or pages to search for. Using `echo`, we can simply create our own content as follows. We run the following command as root and create a very basic welcome page:

```
# echo '<h1>Welcome to our site</h1>' > /var/www/html/index.html
```

The use of single quotes allow tags to be passed as literals.

We can view a page directly; as we have not changed any configuration, there is no need to reload a service. The page should now appear similar to the following screenshot:

We can access this site locally or remotely using the hostname or IP address. We can access the same page using `http://192.168.0.69`, (or which ever IP Address is assigned to your host interface). To access a page remotely, the firewall will need to include `http` and `https` in its `firewalld` rules:

In the following code, we open the HTTP port of port `80` and the HTTPS port of `443`. These are protocols and default ports used to access web servers:

```
$ sudo firewall-cmd --add-service=http --permanent
$ sudo firewall-cmd --add-service=https --permanent
$ sudo firewall-cmd --reload
```

As an administrator of the web server, we are not necessarily going to be the developer on the web content, but we can show that the web server is working with the configuration.

Configuring the DocumentRoot directory

The DocumentRoot directory should be readable by the httpd service. The account used by a service is listed in the httpd.conf. Default accounts that are used with corresponding directives are shown in the following commands:

User apache

Group apache

In an ideal world, the permissions on the /var/www/html directory would be 2750 in an octal notation or rwx r_s _ in a symbolic notation. Setting up a group special bit on a directory ensures that all new content in a directory will be owned by the group owner of the directory. In this way, we do not have to grant any permission to others; as long as the directory is owned by the apache group, files will be accessible to that group.

Firstly, we will set up the group ownership for this directory. We will use the -R option as we have already created the index page after this directory, as shown in the following command:

```
$ sudo chgrp -R apache /var/www/html
```

Now, we will set up the group special bit on the directory; this ensures all new files and directories created in this structure will be owned by the apache group:

```
$ sudo chmod g+s /var/www/html/
```

Finally, we will remove permissions granted to others, helping secure the content as follows:

```
$ sudo chmod -R o= /var/www/html/
```

Although this is not entirely necessary, configuring this at the outset can save work later when perhaps better security is required. With the `httpd.conf`, we also have a directory block that configures the access and options for the `DocumentRoot`. The following screenshot shows the directory block associated with the `DocumentRoot` directory:

```
<Directory "/var/www/html">
      Options Indexes FollowSymLinks
      AllowOverride None
      Require all granted
</Directory>
```

The `Directory` block appears similar to an XML-based data. This uses an opening tag and sets the target directory therein. This block is closed with the `</Directory>` tag:

Options Indexes FollowSymLinks

The `Indexes` option allows the creation of an index page. This option lists the contents of a directory if the name of a page is not included in the URL accessed by a client and no `index.html` exists. This is perhaps great for a downloads directory, alleviating the need for you to create a page linking it to all the available downloads; however, at `DocumentRoot`, we probably do not want this setting because it may pose a security risk.

The `FollowSymLinks` option is probably self-explanatory, which allows you to follow the path of symbolic links. Symbolic links are pointers to other files and directories in a filesystem.

The `AllowOverride` directive specifies settings that can be used from the user control `.htaccess` file. It may be the case with virtual hosts that the administrator does not have access to the web server's configuration file because they are just renting space on the web server. They can effect configurations by uploading an `.htaccess` file to the root of the directory to which the `Directory` block pertains. As the main server administrator, you can control the settings that can be read; here, we allow no settings to be read even if the `.htaccess` file is present:

AllowOverride None

The final setting here is new to Apache 2.4 and replaces the `Allow from` / `Deny from` directive in Apache 2.2 and earlier versions:

Require all granted

The default setting is equivalent to the `Allow from all` setting in Apache 2.2.

If required, you can adjust the host access with a configuration similar to the following commands:

```
Require 192.168.0.0/24
Require 127.0.0.1
```

The preceding access control will only allow access to the localhost and the 192.168.0 network to the associated Directory block.

We will change the configuration setting by editing the /etc/httpd/conf/httpd. conf file. Once we locate the correct Directory block for /var/www/html, we will remove the Index option and leave it as follows:

```
Options FollowSymLinks
```

These changes should be saved, but we need to look at how we can check our settings before attempting to restart the server.

Controlling the Apache web service

When we are ready to test the changes made, we can perform a pre-flight check with the following command:

```
# apachectl configtest
```

You may receive an error message reporting that the hostname could not be resolved. This is a warning and is okay for the moment. The warning is shown in the following screenshot:

```
[root@redhat7 conf]# apachectl configtest
AH00557: httpd: apr_sockaddr_info_get() failed for redhat7.tup.com
AH00558: httpd: Could not reliably determine the server's fully qualified domain name, using 127.0.0.1. Set the
'ServerName' directive globally to suppress this message
Syntax OK
```

The Syntax Ok message at the end is what we want to see; with this, we know that we can restart the web server. Issuing a reload command to the service will force a graceful restart; wait for the active connections to complete before the restart is initiated:

```
$ sudo systemctl reload httpd
```

The effect of the change is limited because we have allowed the local network access and the localhost. Removing the indexes option has no effect while the index.html page is present. If we remove the index.html page, we will receive access forbidden messages because the system will not generate the page. This is important to set because it removes the ability of hackers to be able to retrieve directory listings of our web server.

Setting up the server name

We also need to tidy up the warning about our server's name. This is controlled using the `ServerName` directive in the `httpd.conf`. Adding the `ServerName` directive at the top of the file will resolve the issue:

```
ServerName web.theurbanpenguin.com
```

To completely restart the service, we will use the following command:

```
$ sudo systemctl restart httpd
```

Setting up a custom error page

If we try to access a page on the server that does not exist, the viewer will get a standard `page not found` message. We can make the process a little more controlled and user-friendly by adding our own custom pages.

Within the global section of the `httpd.conf`, we can add the following directive to handle the `404 Page Not Found` message. This global section can affect all directory blocks, but we can add the following directive just to a single directory block if required. Adding the code document for a 404 error will just affect that particular error, but we can add other codes as and when required:

```
ErrorDocument 404 /404.html
```

We can reload the server using the following command:

```
$ sudo systemctl reload httpd
```

Now, when an incorrect page is accessed, the viewer will be shown the custom error page we have created: `404.html`. This page should be created in the `DocumentRoot` because we have used the `/404.html` syntax. If we have many custom pages, we will most likely create an `error` directory in `DocumentRoot` and then reference the page as `/error/404.html`.

Loading modules

Red Hat has moved away from loading modules in the standard `httpd.conf` file. In the previous release of Red Hat (version 6), the configuration file would have been littered with many `LoadModule` directives.

These modules are now loaded via the configuration files in `/etc/httpd/conf.modules.d/`. In this way, the main configuration file is less cluttered and it's easier to drop additional configuration files as and when required.

To view the currently loaded modules from Command Prompt, use the following command:

```
$ sudo httpd -M
```

We can see that we have many modules loaded. We can pipe the output to the wc command to count the lines. Using the RHEL 7.1 demonstration system, the output is 82:

```
$ sudo httpd -M | wc -l
```

With the original output, we should be able to see that the userdir_module is loaded. If we do not need to support user home directories on the web server, we do not need this module. To load this module, the LoadModule directive referencing this Apache module is set in the /etc/httpd/conf.modules.d/00-base.conf file. To ensure that it is not loaded on future restarts of the web server, comment the line that reads as follows:

```
LoadModule userdir_module modules/mod_userdir.so
```

With the line now commented, you will need to restart the web server, but when you check the loaded modules, you should be able to verify that the userdir_module is not loaded.

Virtual servers

Apache has the capability to support multiple sites from the same server instance. This gives great flexibility, and at the same time, ease of management. This flexibility is known as virtual hosting. There are three basic ways of running virtual hosting with Apache:

Name-based	This uses different names for each site and a common IP address, probably the most popular form of virtual hosting
IP-based	This uses a different IP address for each site
Port-based	This uses individual port numbers for each site

We will look at all three of the methods and configurations within the httpd.conf required to implement each method.

Name-based

Name-based virtual hosting has been made possible with the introduction of HTTP protocol version 1.1, also known as HTTP/1.1. When a browser is only capable of HTTP/1.0, a protocol tries to load a web page; it goes through the following steps:

1. Resolves `theurbanpinguin.org` hostname to an IP address.
2. Connects to the resolved IP address over TCP protocol and port `80`.
3. Requests `/index.html` page.

    Therefore, only one website (defined by its domain name) can be hosted at any given IP address. If you direct another domain name—such as `theboldeagle.net`—to the same IP address, a user navigating to a URL will see exactly the same as the user navigating to URL because the web server cannot distinguish between these two requests.

    When the HTTP/1.1 protocol and the HTTP/1.1 capable browser sends a domain name to the web server along with the document path, this is how the next step (step 3) looks:

4. Request `/index.html` page from `theurbanpinguin.org` server.

It's now possible to host two or more different sites on the same IP address because the web server can distinguish between different domain names, as domain names now form a part of the HTTP request.

All contemporary web browsers support HTTP/1.1. There are two aspects to name-based virtual hosting, which we will now look at.

The name resolution

All the names for a site need to be mapped to the same IP address either via DNS or a localhost file. If any of the names are used in the system, the returned IP address will always be the same. The redirection of the incoming request to the correct location in the filesystem is handled by the `httpd` service and the incoming `http` header.

The Apache configuration

The key to name-based virtual hosting lies in the `httpd.conf` file in a block directive:

```
<VirtualHost virtual host IP>
.
.
.
</VirtualHost>
```

Almost any Apache entry is valid here including the `ErrorDocument` directive that we saw earlier. We have included the most typical entries in the following example:

```
<VirtualHost *.80>
    ServerName www.packtpub.com
    ServerAdmin andrew@example.com
    DocumentRoot "/var/www/packt/html"
    ErrorLog "/var/www/packt/logs/packt_error"
    TransferLog "/var/www/packt/logs/packt_access"
</VirtualHost>
```

Using the preceding example, we will be directed to the web pages in `/var/www/packt/html`, if we use the URL of `https://www.packtpub.com/` while accessing the server's IP address.

In order for Apache to find the correct entries for virtual hosts, we must tell it which IP address they are aliases for. However, it's not enough to define a virtual host using the previous block because Apache does not allow name-based virtual hosting by default. To make name-based virtual hosts work, this is done using the `NameVirtualHost` directive, which needs to be included in the `httpd.conf` file. This directive must be in the main server section:

```
NameVirtualHost *:80
```

IP-based

The IP addresses used must be bound to the main RHEL server. Within the Apache `httpd.conf`, we again use the `VirtualHost` block, but we do not need to set the `NameVirtualHost` directive. Instead of specifying `*:80` as IP and port selectors of `VirtualHost` block, we will use a real IP address that the Apache server listens to, that is, IP address assigned to one of the interfaces of the machine that the Apache server is running on. The following commands show a possible configuration we can add to the main `httpd.conf`:

```
<VirtualHost 192.168.0.221:80>
    ServerName www.example.com
    ServerAdmin andrew@example.com
    DocumentRoot "/var/www/example/html"
</VirtualHost>
```

Apache listens for incoming connections on all interfaces of the machine by default, so it should be enough just to specify an IP address of one of the interfaces in the `<VirtualHost>` opening directive. However, to be doubly sure that Apache listens to the right interface, the following command should be included in the main section of the `httpd.conf` file.

```
Listen 192.168.0.221:80
```

Using the previous example, when we access the host with the IP address `192.168.0.221`, we will be redirected to web pages in `/var/www/example/html`.

Port-based

There is only one aspect to port-based virtual hosting: the Apache configuration with the main `httpd.conf`. An example is as follows:

```
<VirtualHost 192.168.0.220:7070>
  ServerName www.example.com
  ServerAdmin andrew@example.com
  DocumentRoot "/var/www/example/html"
</VirtualHost>
```

Using the previous example, when we access the port `7070` on the Apache host with the IP address of `192.168.0.220`, we will be redirected to web pages in `/var/www/example/html`.

Within all `VirtualHost` blocks, we can expect a `Directory` block in addition to the code we have shown so far. In this way, options and access control lists can be correctly set for each virtual host.

Automating virtual hosts

If we create a template file for a virtual host, we can easily drop new virtual hosts using a script. First, we need a template file that is similar to the following commands:

```
<VirtualHost *:80>
  ServerAdmin webmaster@dummy-host.example.com
  ServerName dummy-host.example.com
  DocumentRoot /var/www/dummy-host.example.com
  ErrorLog /var/log/httpd/dummy-host.example.com-error_log
  CustomLog /var/log/httpd/dummy-host.example.com-access_log
  UseCanonicalName Off
  ServerSignature On
  <Directory "/var/www/vhosts/dummy-host.example.com">
    Options Indexes FollowSymLinks
```

```
        AllowOverride None
        Require all granted
    </Directory>
</VirtualHost>
```

If this file is saved as /etc/httpd/conf.d/template, it will not be used as a configuration as it does not end in .conf. We can use it as a template with a script similar to the following commands:

```
#!/bin/bash
CONFDIR=/etc/httpd/conf.d
WEBDIR=/var/www/
mkdir -p $WEBDIR/$1
sed s/"dummy-host.example.com"/$1/g \
$CONFDIR/template > $CONFDIR/$1.conf
echo "This is a website in construction for $1" \
> $WEBDIR/$1/index.html
systemctl reload httpd
```

If the script is called /root/vhost.sh, we can run it as follows:

```
# /root/vhost.sh www.example.com
```

The preceding script will create a new configuration and replace dummy-host.example.com with www.example.com.

Summary

This chapter introduced you to the Apache HTTPD service that runs on RHEL 7.1. We looked at the ServerRoot being /etc/httpd and the DocumentRoot being /var/www/html. With the basics in place, you learned how to configure a server with custom error pages and virtual hosts.

In the next chapter, we will look at SELinux in detail and try to leave you with the idea that you can implement SELinux without affecting your service delivery in a negative way. In fact, the word negative is far from the truth. SELinux will deliver you a secure and robust platform so that you can deploy public-facing services without any fear of compromise, adding **Mandatory Access Controls (MAC)** to the existing, but weaker **DAC (Discretionary Access Controls)**.

10

Securing the System with SELinux

All too often you will find a tutorial or a blog that will advise you to disable SELinux. This will be in order to get a particular feature of vservice working. In many cases, people have to do is to follow the blog or tutorial instructions because very little is known about SELinux. The aim of this chapter is to provide you a remedy to this and help you become more familiar with how SELinux works. This chapter will provide you with the protection that SELinux provides so that next time you are better equipped to deal with a blog that metaphorically advises you to leave the keys in the ignition of your parked car.

In this chapter, we will cover the following topics:

- What is SELinux
- Understanding SELinux
- Working with the targeted policy type
- Policies in SELinux
- SELinux tools
- Troubleshooting SELinux

What is SELinux

SELinux is a **MAC (Mandatory Access Control)** system working together with the existing **DAC (Discretionary Access Control)** list we are familiar with, such as the file permissions list.

SELinux can only restrict permissions; it cannot add permissions. If the DAC does not allow access, SELinux cannot allow.

In order to work with labeled objects, access is granted based on these labels and controlled via policies. All objects—such as users, processes, and files—have labels. The label that you have or (more often) the process that you run must match the label supplied to the resource that you need to access. In simple terms, think of this like bathrooms; humans with the label MEN have access to the bathroom labeled MEN. In Linux terms, the Apache web server process is labeled as `httpd_t` and can access files with the `httpd_sys_content_t` label. In this way, your system is protected against a rogue or **pwned** (compromised) web server as the scope of files that has access to it is limited by SELinux.

SELinux is maintained by Red Hat, NSA, and Secure Computing, so it has a rich pedigree. It comprises of four major components that we will investigate in this chapter:

* Modes
* Labels
* Policy types
* Policy packages

To help you work with SELinux, we will install some additional packages. These RPM packages are shown in the following command line. For ease of layout, we have added line breaks:

```
$ sudo yum install policycoreutils-python policycoreutils-gui \
 setools-console setools-gui setroubleshoot \
 setroubleshoot-server
```

Understanding SELinux

Let's start pulling the covers off SELinux and discover a little more about what makes these controls work, starting with SELinux modes.

Modes

To begin with, we will discuss three modes that we can run with SELinux. These modes are illustrated for you in the following figure:

The disabled mode

When SELinux is disabled, SELinux is not used and the objects are NOT labeled. In the disabled mode, we rely solely on the original DAC. If we later need to enable SELinux, the boot process is lengthened because all the objects need to be relabeled again. Disabling SELinux completely like this is probably not a good idea, but should it be required, it can be set in the `/etc/selinux/config` file by changing the following line:

```
SELINUX=disabled
```

One reason this is not a great idea is that a reboot is required for this to take effect. As mentioned before, files need to be relabeled if SELinux is enabled later. We can force a relabel if all filesystem objects are running by running the the following command:

```
# fixfiles relabel
```

Alternatively, we can create the `/.autorelabel` file, as shown in the following command:

```
# touch /.autorelabel
```

The permissive mode

If you are having issues with a service and want to check whether SELinux is a possible culprit, you may prefer to set SELinux in the permissive mode. In this way, SELinux is still enabled and the objects maintain their labels; however, events are not blocked, but logged to the `/var/log/audit/audit.log` file.

To enter the permissive mode, we can perform this while the system is running without performing a reboot on your system. The following line illustrates how this is achieved:

```
# setenforce Permissive
```

If the change is made in this way, then on a reboot, the permissive mode is applied from `/etc/selinux/config`. To set the mode permanently to permissive, we should set the permissive mode in the following line:

```
SELINUX=permissive
```

Although I do feel that setting the mode to permissive is acceptable as a quick and simple test, the more you know about SELinux, the less likely you are to move from the Enforcing mode where your protection is guaranteed. In this chapter, you will learn how to correct issues and even add a process to be permissive rather than the whole system.

It's also possible to set permissive or enforcing modes via the boot loader, adding the following commands at the end of the kernel line (where 0 is off or permissive and 1 is on or enforcing):

```
enforcing=0
enforcing=1
```

The enforcing mode

The enforcing mode is very similar to the permissive mode, where you can switch between permissive and enforcing on the command line with the setenforce command. As the name suggests, SELinux is enforced in this mode and reported to the log file as well.

To interrogate your current SELinux mode, you can issue the getenforce command. If you have installed additional tools, you will also be able to run the sestatus command, which is part of the policycoreutils package. This command displays the current mode and the mode from the configuration file; the output of sestatus is shown in the following screenshot:

```
[root@centos7 ~]# sestatus
SELinux status:                 enabled
SELinuxfs mount:                /sys/fs/selinux
SELinux root directory:         /etc/selinux
Loaded policy name:             targeted
Current mode:                   enforcing
Mode from config file:          enforcing
Policy MLS status:              enabled
Policy deny_unknown status:     allowed
Max kernel policy version:      28
```

Labels

As mentioned previously, when SELinux is in the permissive or enforcing mode, all objects — such as files, users, and processes — have labels. When accessing resources, these labels are compared to see whether the match is compatible.

Each label consists of four colon delimited values:

- The SELinux user
- The SELinux role
- The SELinux type
- The SELinux level

In general, a level is only used in very secure government environments, where the secrecy level of the user must match the secrecy level of the document or resource. The idea here is that the President will be able to read anything, but only write to documents that match his security level. This even prevents him from writing to documents holding a lower security level. Of course, this can be read by lower authorized people and can perhaps be a security breach.

Using the ls command, we can list the label of a file using the -z option. The following command is an example of listing the SELinux label from the /etc/hosts file:

```
$ ls -Z /etc/hosts
```

The output should look similar to the following screenshot:

```
[andrew@rhlabs ~]$ ls -Z /etc/hosts
-rw-r--r--. root root system_u:object_r:net_conf_t:s0  /etc/hosts
[andrew@rhlabs ~]$
```

After reading the label, we can determine the following values that are read from left to right from the previous screenshot:

The SELinux user	system_u
The SELinux role	object_r
The SELinux type	net_conf_t
The SELinux level	s0

To read a label from a Linux user perspective, we can use the id -Z <username> command. The following screenshot shows this for the currently logged in user, where the <username> field can be left blank:

```
[andrew@rhlabs ~]$ id -Z
unconfined_u:unconfined_r:unconfined_t:s0-s0:c0.c1023
[andrew@rhlabs ~]$
```

Similarly, we can examine the label of a process using the -z option with the ps command, as shown in the following command:

```
$ ps -eZ | grep ssh
```

```
[andrew@rhlabs ~]$ ps -eZ | grep ssh
system_u:system_r:sshd_t:s0-s0:c0.c1023 7952 ? 00:00:00 sshd
```

Policy types

The default SELinux policy type is targeted, but three policy types are listed as follows:

- Minimum
- Targeted
- MLS

They are all contained in packages that match the `selinux-policy-minimum`, `selinux-policy-targeted`, and `selinux-policy-mls` names.

Minimum

As the name suggests, this is designed as a minimum configuration for SELinux. As strange as may sound, this is for situations where you want to target just one service, such as the Apache web server. Starting with the basics, it's easy to include additional policies in your `Minimum` type. The following command shows how we can use `semodule` to add the Apache policy:

```
# semodule -i /usr/share/selinux/minimum/Apache.pp.bz2
```

To configure SELinux to use the `Minimum` policy, we set the `SELINUXTYPE` directive using the `/etc/selinux/config` file:

```
SELINUXTYPE=minimum
```

Targeted

This is the default policy type; by default, many policies are included. On the demo system, there are 395 policies installed other than the basic policy. We can use `semodule` to list all modules:

```
# semodule -l
```

MLS

The multi-level security or MLS policy type will allow you to add additional levels of security. These can be interrogated from labels to help you control access to resources. This is generally used only in high security deployments. Outside of MLS, the level element of a label is not used. To enable MLS, the `/etc/selinux/config` file is configured with the following directive:

```
SELINUXTYPE=mls
```

Policies

Once policies are installed, individual policies are installed in the appropriate policy type directory; for the default targeted policy, enter `/etc/selinux/targeted/modules/active/modules/`. Policy files have the `.pp` suffix.

Working with the targeted policy type

The default policy type is targeted. As such, most SELinux deployments will work with this policy type. In the case of the targeted policy type, the primary attribute from the label used for enforcement is `type`. For this reason, the targeted policy type is often known as TE or `type` enforcement. The following image highlights the importance of the type attribute of a label in the targeted policy type:

Using the `seinfo` command, which is part of the `setools-console` package, we can display specific information about the current SELinux environment. Let's take a look at the available types that we can work with. To list all types, we will use the following command:

```
# seinfo -t
```

Wow, there are a lot. If we count them, we have around 4500 on RHEL 7; on RHEL 6, there were 3500. These two figures are just a simple illustration of how much the SELinux product is growing and its continued uptake, but Linux software developers.

We can also see how to import the type attribute in a label with the user attribute:

```
# seinfo -u
```

Here, the numbers are not so impressive; it's just 8. These are not Linux users, but SELinux users; Linux users can be mapped to SELinux users to help control access to resources. To display any mapping, we can use `semanage`, as follows:

```
# semanage login -l
```

Without any mapping being set up, we will see that the root is mapped to `unconfined_u` because this is the default. This setting means that all other user accounts without any specific mapping will be mapped to the `unconfined_u` SELinux user, which means that we are ignoring the user attribute in the label as it's unconfined on SELinux. Similarly, let's look at the ROLE attribute using `seinfo`:

```
# seinfo -r
```

The output should indicate 14 roles; again, this is not a large number. The role attribute is not heavily used in the targeted policy type.

Unconfined domains

The TYPE attribute is often referred to as the DOMAIN when set on a process; remember that we can view the SELinux label of a running process using the following process status command:

```
$ ps -eZ
```

Many processes started in a user space will also be unconfined perhaps to the TYPE attribute set to `unconfined_t`. If processes started in the user space are generally unconfined, we can say that services, especially network facing services, will be enforced in some way and this is very much representative of why SELinux is here: to protect against attack from exposure to a network. It's not only the `aunconfined_t` tag that is unconfined by SELinux. To display all unconfined types or domains, we can use `seinfo` running as root again as follows:

```
# seinfo -aunconfined_domain_type  -x
```

The `-a` option tells `seinfo` that we are searching for an attribute; this attribute needs to be pushed up next to the option with no additional white spaces. The `-x` attribute expands to show all TYPEs that have the attribute, rather than just listing the attribute itself. The output should confirm that it is mainly domains that will be non-network facing that are unconfined, such as `bootloader_t`.

The following screenshot displays the start of the output from my system. In total, there were 86 unconfined domains; this is not bad considering that we started with 4500 types in all:

```
[andrew@rhlabs ~]$ sudo seinfo -aunconfined_domain_type -x
   unconfined_domain_type
       sosreport_t
       bootloader_t
       devicekit_power_t
```

When policies are enforced, the default level of access is denied; this means that rules must exist in the policy package in order to allow access to users, roles, or types. Having the default access denied ensures security if a given scenario is not considered; on the flip side, this also means that access needs to be added if your given scenario has not been considered. A level of administration may be required to tune the environment to your needs; however, once set up, you have a secure system that will continue to run reliably with a lessened exposure to risk.

Of course, although the default auction in a policy is to deny access to a resource, there are many thousands of `allow rules` supplied within these polices by default. Using the `sesearch` command, we can display them; sending results to the `wc` command can count the number of rules. The following commands illustrate this:

```
# sesearch --allow #display all allow rules
# sesearch --allow | grep wc -l #count the output
```

On my system, there are over 100,000 rules created by default. If we want to look at this in a little more detail, we can search for the `httpd_sys_content_t` string. There are many rules with this label, but if we look at just one, the easiest is to consider is the last one with the command tail. Here, we can see that access is granted to resources with `httpd_sys_content_t` to process with the `ftpd_t` label. In simple terms, the FTP server has access to your website content, as shown in the following command:

```
# sesearch --allow | grep httpd_sys_content_t | tail -n 1
allow ftpd_t httpd_sys_content_t : dir { getattr search open } ;
```

Now, we have a little more understanding of the default targeted policy type, so let's take a look at how to use some of the tools and see SELinux at work.

SELinux tools

Let's take a look at SELinux tools.

chcon and restorecon

Two of the main tools that we can use to help manage SELinux are `chcon` and `restorecon`. The `chcon` command helps to change the SELinux context or TYPE of what will most often be a single or perhaps sometimes a few files that can be referenced easily together with some form of wildcard. The `restorecon` command can be used to reset a file or directory and its contents to their default SELinux context. These default settings for directories are stored in the `/etc/selinux/targeted/contexts/files/file-context` file.

With `grep`, we can search for `httpd_sys_content_t`, whereas in the output, we should see the default label for files under `/var/www`. This is the directory were we would expect to find web server content:

```
# grep httpd_sys_content_t \
/etc/selinux/targeted/contexts/files/file_contexts
```

The output of the preceding command is as follows:

```
/var/www(/.*)? system_u:object_r:httpd_sys_content_t:s0
```

We can now try to break the system by changing the SELinux context of the `index.html` page. We can do this with the `chcon` command as follows:

```
# chcon -t user_home_t /var/www/html/index.html
```

Now, if we navigate to the website using the `localhost` URL, we should have an access denied message of some description. This is because we have set the TYPE of the file to `user_home_t`; access is not permitted to the `httpd_t` context in which the web server runs. The following screenshot shows the use of `chcon` and the subsequent denial message:

```
[root@redhat7 ~]# chcon -t user_home_t /var/www/html/index.html
[root@redhat7 ~]# wget localhost
--2015-04-17 16:30:31--  http://localhost/
Resolving localhost (localhost)... ::1, 127.0.0.1
Connecting to localhost (localhost)|::1|:80... connected.
HTTP request sent, awaiting response... 403 Forbidden
2015-04-17 16:30:31 ERROR 403: Forbidden.
```

Of course, we can fix this manually by setting the type back to `httpd_sys_content_t` using `chcon`; however, if we are unsure of the correct context, we can run the `restorecon` command, as shown in the following command line:

```
# restorecon /var/www/html/index.html
```

Accessing the web page should now work. Technically, we can achieve the same effect as achieved with `restorecon` by relabeling the complete filesystem at reboot by creating the `/.autorelabel` file; as you can imagine, this is a little overkill and will take a while. The effect of this though is to run `restorecon` across the complete filesystem.

Boolean values

There are also simple Boolean values that we can toggle on and off as required, to help tune our system to work the way we need to match our environment. On the RHEL 7.1 system used in the book, we have 294 Boolean values that can be adjusted. We can display these with the simple getsebool command:

```
# getsebool -a
```

We will drill down a little further and list those associated with the httpd process. We can see this in the following screenshot:

```
[root@redhat7 ~]# getsebool -a | grep httpd
httpd_anon_write --> off
httpd_builtin_scripting --> on
httpd_can_check_spam --> off
httpd_can_connect_ftp --> off
httpd_can_connect_ldap --> off
httpd_can_connect_mythtv --> off
httpd_can_connect_zabbix --> off
httpd_can_network_connect --> off
httpd_can_network_connect_cobbler --> off
httpd_can_network_connect_db --> off
httpd_can_network_memcache --> off
```

To change a Boolean value, we can use the setsebool command which can be a temporary or permanent fix. The use of the -P option is required if we want the change the Boolean value to be permanent. This also will take a while because the active policy is written to and recompiled.

If we return to the earlier setting where the index.html page was set with context to user home directories, we can remedy with setsebool. If the situation was not appropriate to change the context, for example, if we need to host user home directories on the web server temporarily until the next boot, we can use the following command:

```
# setsebool httpd_read_user_content on
```

If we need this to be set permanently, we will use the following command:

```
# setsebool -P httpd_read_user_content on
```

The temporary setting is shown in the following screenshot. It also shows successful access to the web page that still has the incorrect context set:

```
[root@redhat7 ~]# setsebool httpd_read_user_content on
[root@redhat7 ~]# wget localhost
--2015-04-17 16:35:50--  http://localhost/
Resolving localhost (localhost)... ::1, 127.0.0.1
Connecting to localhost (localhost)|::1|:80... connected.
HTTP request sent, awaiting response... 200 OK
Length: 29 [text/html]
Saving to: 'index.html.1'

100%[=======================================>] 29          --.-K/s   in 0s

2015-04-17 16:35:50 (1.65 MB/s) - 'index.html.1' saved [29/29]
```

Using these Booleans can go a long way in resolving issues you may have with SELinux.

Troubleshooting SELinux

Let's take a look at different ways of troubleshooting SELinux.

The log file

If we were left uncertain as to the problem that was causing errors that we encountered before with the web server, then our troubleshooting should always start with log files. For SELinux, this is the /var/log/audit/audit.log file. Logging in from SELinux will be marked as **AVC (Access Vector Cache)**. We can search the log file with grep using something similar to the following command:

```
# grep AVC /var/log/audit/audit.log
```

However, more appropriately, there is also the ausearch command that we can use. If an error has just occurred, we can use the recent time start code to help reduce returned results. This is a shortcut for displaying errors within the last 10 minutes:

```
# ausearch -m avc -ts recent
```

Other than this, we can supply an actual time, date, or both. In the following example, we will use 16:00 as the starting time to search. In the absence of the date, today's date is implied as follows:

```
# ausearch -m avc -ts 16:00
```

Taking a look at the output from the command in the following screenshot, we can see that the process and resource have incompatible labels:

```
[root@redhat7 ~]# ausearch -m avc -ts 16:00
----
time->Fri Apr 17 16:30:31 2015
type=SYSCALL msg=audit(1429284631.400:156): arch=c000003e syscall=2 success=no e
xit=-13 a0=7fa72c9cb738 a1=80000 a2=0 a3=7fff25c7ca40 items=0 ppid=3542 pid=3937
 auid=4294967295 uid=48 gid=48 euid=48 suid=48 fsuid=48 egid=48 sgid=48 fsgid=48
 tty=(none) ses=4294967295 comm="httpd" exe="/usr/sbin/httpd" subj=system_u:syst
em_r:httpd_t:s0 key=(null)
type=AVC msg=audit(1429284631.400:156): avc:  denied  { read } for  pid=3937 com
m="httpd" name="index.html" dev="dm-1" ino=37036209 scontext=system_u:system_r:h
ttpd_t:s0 tcontext=unconfined_u:object_r:user_home_t:s0 tclass=file
```

The audit2allow command

Now, even after having checked the log file, you still may not be entirely clear about the cause of the problem or its possible fix. For help, you can try the `audit2allow` command. If used with the `-w` option, an explanation of the problem along with possible solutions are included in the output. We still examine the log, but this time we will pipe the output through to the `audit2allow` command as follows:

```
# ausearch -m avc -ts 16:00 | audit2allow -w
```

The output from the test system looked like this when we had reset the original Boolean value:

```
[root@redhat7 ~]# setsebool httpd_read_user_content off
[root@redhat7 ~]# ausearch -m avc -ts 16:00 | audit2allow -w
type=AVC msg=audit(1429284631.400:156): avc:  denied  { read } for  pid=3937 com
m="httpd" name="index.html" dev="dm-1" ino=37036209 scontext=system_u:system_r:h
ttpd_t:s0 tcontext=unconfined_u:object_r:user_home_t:s0 tclass=file

        Was caused by:
        The boolean httpd_read_user_content was set incorrectly.
        Description:
        Allow httpd to read user content

        Allow access by executing:
        # setsebool -P httpd_read_user_content 1
[root@redhat7 ~]#
```

We can see that the suggestion matches the Boolean setting we had previously shown works. If the problem was more complex than changing a Boolean value, we could create a new policy package using the -M option. Then using `semodule`, we would import the `.pp` file as follows:

```
# ausearch -m avc -ts 16:00 | audit2allow -M web.local
# semodule -i web.local.pp
```

Permissive domains

We can see that there are some pretty powerful tools designed to help with our SELinux deployments, but if all else fails, there is another option called **Permissive domains**.

Rather than setting the SELinux mode to Permissive, we can turn the Permissive status on for just a single domain or process context. By default, permissive domains are enabled and these are known as built-in permissive domains. Domains that we add are customized domains.

Although the web server is a major network facing attach vector, maybe if we cannot get SELinux working with `httpd`, but we do not want to risk SELinux disabled for the rest of the system. We can turn on the permissive behavior for `httpd_t` using the following command:

```
# semanage permissive -a httpd_t
```

Should we need to remove this behavior later, we can reverse it with:

```
# semanage permissive -d httpd_t
```

In both cases, we will write to the active policy; this will take a little time.

Summary

In this chapter, you learned how to manage SELinux. I certainly hope that you have a much fuller understanding of the mechanism involved. The aim of SELinux is to protect a system, especially where network-facing services are involved. Disabling or setting the Permissive mode for SELinux is, in general, the wrong approach. With this, you should now be be able to choose the correct solution.

In the next chapter, we will look at the new firewalling mechanism included on RHEL 7 and the improvements made from the standard `IPtables` mechanism used in the past. Again, we hope that we can convince you of the benefits of `firewalld` and keep the service enabled.

11
Network Security with firewalld

The default user interface for `netfilter`, the kernel-based firewall, on RHEL7 is `firewalld`. Administrators now have a choice to use `firewalld` or `iptables` to manage firewalls. Underlying either process, we can still implement the kernel-based `netfilter` firewall. The frontend command to this new interface is `firewall-cmd`. The main benefit this offers is the ability to refresh the `netfilter` setting when the firewall is running. This is not possible with the `iptables` interface; additionally, we are able to use zone management. This enables us to have different firewall configurations, which depends on the network we are connected to.

In this chapter, we will be cover the following topics:

- The firewall status
- Routing
- The zone management
- The source management
- Firewall rules using services
- Firewall rules using ports
- Masquerading and the network address translation
- Using rich rules
- Implementing direct rules
- Reverting to iptables

The firewall status

The firewall service can provide protection for your RHEL system and services from other hosts on the local network or Internet. Although firewalling is often maintained on the border routers to your network, additional protection can be provided by host-based firewalls, such as the `netfilter` firewall on the Linux kernel. The `netfilter` firewall on RHEL 7 can be implemented via the `iptables` or `firewalld` service, with the latter being the default.

The status of the `firewalld` service can be interrogated in a normal manner using the `systemctl` command. This will provide a verbose output if the service is running. This will include the **PID (process ID)** of `firewalld` along with recent log messages. The following is a command extract along with a screenshot of the output from RHEL7.1:

```
# systemctl status firewalld
```

```
[root@redhat7 ~]# systemctl status firewalld
firewalld.service - firewalld - dynamic firewall daemon
   Loaded: loaded (/usr/lib/systemd/system/firewalld.service; disabled)
   Active: active (running) since Sat 2015-04-25 08:42:17 BST; 50min ago
 Main PID: 51527 (firewalld)
   CGroup: /system.slice/firewalld.service
           └─51527 /usr/bin/python -Es /usr/sbin/firewalld --nofork --nopid

Apr 25 08:42:17 redhat7.tup.com systemd[1]: Started firewalld - dynamic fire....
Hint: Some lines were ellipsized, use -l to show in full.
[root@redhat7 ~]#
```

If you just need a quick check with a less verbose output, make use of the `firewall-cmd` command. This is the main administrative tool used to manage `firewalld`. The `--state` option will provide all that you need, as shown in the following screenshot:

```
[root@redhat7 ~]# firewall-cmd --state
running
[root@redhat7 ~]#
```

If `firewalld` was not active, the output would show as `not running`.

Routing

Although not strictly necessary for a firewall, you may need to implement routing on your RHEL7 system. Often, this will be associated with multi-homed systems with more than one network interface card; however, this is not a requirement of network routing, which allows packets to be forwarded to the correct destination network. Network routing is enabled in `procfs` in the `/proc/sys/net/ipv4/ip_forward` file. If this file contains a value of `0`, then routing is disabled; if it has a value of `1`, routing is enabled. This can be set using the `echo` command as follows:

```
# echo 1 > /proc/sys/net/ipv4/ip_forward
```

However, this is then turned on until the next reboot when the routing will revert to the configured setting. To make this setting permanent traditionally, the `/etc/sysctl.conf` file has been used. It's now recommended to add you own configurations to `/etc/sysctl.d/`. Here is an example of this:

```
# echo "net.ipv4.ip_forward = 1" > /etc/sysctl.d/ipforward.conf
```

This will create a file and set its directive. To make this setting effective prior to the next reboot, we can make use of the `sysctl` command, as shown in the following command:

```
# sysctl -p /etc/sysctl.d/ipforward.conf
```

This can also be seen in the following screenshot. Here, you can see that we read from the running configuration in `procfs` before implementing a change. It also shows the change to the running `procfs`:

```
[root@redhat7 ~]# cat /proc/sys/net/ipv4/ip_forward
0
[root@redhat7 ~]# echo "net.ipv4.ip_forward = 1" > /etc/sysctl.d/ipforward.conf
[root@redhat7 ~]# sysctl -p !$
sysctl -p /etc/sysctl.d/ipforward.conf
net.ipv4.ip_forward = 1
[root@redhat7 ~]# cat /proc/sys/net/ipv4/ip_forward
1
[root@redhat7 ~]#
```

Zone management

A new feature you will find in `firewalld` that is more aimed at mobile systems—such as laptops—is the inclusion of zones. However, these zones can be equally used on a multihomed system, which associates different NICs with appropriate zones. Using zones in either mobile or multihomed systems, firewall rules can be assigned to zones and these rules will be associated with NICs included in that zone. If an interface is not assigned explicitly to a zone, then it will become a part of the default zone. To interrogate the default zone on your system, we can use the `firewall-cmd` command, as shown in the following command line:

```
# firewall-cmd --get-default-zone
```

Should you need to list all the configured zones on your system, the following command can be used:

```
# firewall-cmd --get-zones
```

The following screenshot demonstrates this command and the default zones on RHEL 7.1:

```
[root@redhat7 ~]# firewall-cmd --get-zones
block dmz drop external home internal public trusted work
[root@redhat7 ~]#
```

Perhaps more usefully, we can display zones with interfaces assigned to them; if no assignments have been made, then all the interfaces will be in the public zone. The `--get-active-zones` option will help us with this, as shown in the following command:

```
# firewall-cmd --get-active-zones
```

Should we require a more verbose output, we can list all the zone names, associated rules, and interfaces. The following command demonstrates how this can be achieved:

```
# firewall-cmd --list-all-zones
```

If you need to utilize zones, you can choose the default zone and assign interfaces to specific zones as well. Firstly, assign a new default zone as follows:

```
# firewall-cmd --set-default-zone=work
```

Here, we redirect the default zone to the work zone. In this way, all NICs that have not been explicitly assigned will participate in the work zone. The preceding command should report back with success. Take a look at the following screenshot to see how this works:

```
[root@redhat7 ~]# firewall-cmd --set-default-zone=work
success
```

We can also explicitly assign a zone to an interface as follows:

```
# firewall-cmd --zone=public --change-interface=eno16777736
```

The change made through this command will be temporary until the next reboot; to make it permanent, we will add the --permanent option:

```
# firewall-cmd --zone=public --change-interface=eno16777736 --permanent
```

Making a setting permanent will persist the configuration within the zone file located in the /etc/firewalld/zones/ directory. In our case, the file is /etc/firewalld/zones/public.xml. After having implemented the permanent change as detailed here, we can list the contents of the XML file with the cat command. This is shown in the following screenshot:

```
[root@redhat7 ~]# cat /etc/firewalld/zones/public.xml
<?xml version="1.0" encoding="utf-8"?>
<zone>
  <short>Public</short>
  <description>For use in public areas. You do not trust the other computers on netw
arm your computer. Only selected incoming connections are accepted.</description>
  <interface name="eno16777736"/>
  <service name="dhcpv6-client"/>
  <service name="http"/>
  <service name="ssh"/>
  <service name="https"/>
</zone>
[root@redhat7 ~]#
```

We can either interrogate an individual NIC to view the zone it's associated with or list all interfaces within a zone; the following commands illustrate this:

```
# firewall-cmd --get-zone-of-interface=eno16777736
```

```
# firewall-cmd --zone=public --list-all
```

You can use tab completion to assist with options and arguments with firewall-cmd.

If the supplied zones are not ample or perhaps the names do not work for your naming schemes, it's possible to create your own zones and add interfaces and rules. After adding your zone, you can reload the configuration to allow it to be used immediately as follows:

```
# firewall-cmd --permanent --new-zone=packt
# firewall-cmd --reload
```

The `--reload` option can reload the configuration that allows current connections to continue uninterrupted; whereas the `--complete-reload` option will stop all connections during the process.

Source management

The problem that you may encounter using interfaces assigned to your zones is that it does not differentiate between network addresses. Often, this is not an issue as only one network address is bound to the NIC; however, if you have more than one address bound to the NIC, you may want to implement the `firewalld` source. Like interfaces, sources can be assigned to zones. In the following command, we will add a network range to the `trusted` zone and another range, perhaps on the same NIC to the `public` zone:

```
# firewall-cmd --permanent --zone=trusted --add-source=192.168.1.0/24
# firewall-cmd --permanent --zone=public --add-source=172.17.0.0/16
```

Similar to interfaces, binding a source to a zone will activate that zone and will be listed with the `--get-active-zones` option.

Firewall rules using services

When we think of firewalls, we think of allowing or denial of access to ports. The use of service XML files can ease the port management with one service, perhaps listing multiple ports. The other point to take note of is that `firewalld` daemon's default policy is to deny access, so any access needed has to be explicitly granted to a port associated with a service. To list services that have been allowed on the default zone, we can simply use the `--list-services` option, as shown in the following example:

```
# firewall-cmd --list-services
```

Similarly, we can gain access to services allowed in a specific zone by including the `--zone=` option. This can be seen in the following example:

```
# firewall-cmd --zone=home --list-services
```

The output from this command is shown in the following screenshot. It lists services associated with the home zone:

```
[root@redhat7 ~]# firewall-cmd --list-services --zone=home
dhcpv6-client ipp-client mdns samba-client ssh
[root@redhat7 ~]# █
```

As you start enabling services, you can easily allow a predefined service through a zone. Predefined services are listed as XML files in the /usr/lib/firewalld/ services directory. They are listed in the following screenshot for you to examine:

```
[root@redhat7 ~]# ls /lib/firewalld/services/
amanda-client.xml        http.xml          libvirt.xml       pmwebapis.xml        smtp.xml
bacula-client.xml        imaps.xml         mdns.xml          pmwebapi.xml         ssh.xml
bacula.xml               ipp-client.xml    mountd.xml        pop3s.xml            telnet.xml
dhcpv6-client.xml        ipp.xml           ms-wbt.xml        postgresql.xml       tftp-client.xml
dhcpv6.xml               ipsec.xml         mysql.xml         proxy-dhcp.xml       tftp.xml
dhcp.xml                 kerberos.xml      nfs.xml           radius.xml           transmission-client.xml
dns.xml                  kpasswd.xml       ntp.xml           RH-Satellite-6.xml   vnc-server.xml
ftp.xml                  ldaps.xml         openvpn.xml       rpc-bind.xml         wbem-https.xml
high-availability.xml    ldap.xml          pmcd.xml          samba-client.xml
https.xml                libvirt-tls.xml   pmproxy.xml       samba.xml
[root@redhat7 ~]# █
```

RHEL 7 is representative of a more mature Linux distribution; as such, it recognizes that the need to separate the /usr directory from the root filesystem is depreciated and the /lib, /bin, and /sbin directories are soft-linked to their respective directories after /usr/. Hence, /lib is now the same as /usr/lib. This is illustrated in the following screenshot:

```
[root@redhat7 ~]# ls -l /bin /lib /sbin
lrwxrwxrwx. 1 root root 7 Dec 12 16:03 /bin -> usr/bin
lrwxrwxrwx. 1 root root 7 Dec 12 16:03 /lib -> usr/lib
lrwxrwxrwx. 1 root root 8 Dec 12 16:03 /sbin -> usr/sbin
[root@redhat7 ~]#
```

While defining your own services, you may create XML files within the /etc/ firewalld/services directory. The squid proxy server does not have its own service file, and if we choose to allow this as a service rather than just opening the required port the file would look similar to the /etc/firewalld/services/squid. xml, as follows:

```xml
<?xml version="1.0" encoding="utf-8"?>
<service>
  <short>Squid</short>
  <description>Squid Web Proxy</description>
  <port protocol="tcp" port="3128"/>
</service>
```

Assuming that we are using SELinux in the Enforcing mode, we will need to set the correct context for the new file using the following commands:

```
# cd /etc/firewalld/services
# restorecon squid.xml
```

The permissions on this file should be 640 and it will be set using the following command:

```
# chmod 640 /etc/firewalld/services/squid.xml
```

The output of ls -lZ should read similar to the following screenshot, where we display the correct SELinux context and permission:

```
[root@redhat7 services]# pwd
/etc/firewalld/services
[root@redhat7 services]# ls -lZ squid.xml
-rw-r-----. root root unconfined_u:object_r:firewalld_etc_rw_t:s0 squid.xml
[root@redhat7 services]# █
```

Having defined the new service now or using pre-existing services, we can add them to a zone. If we are using the default zone, this is achieved simply with the following commands. Note that we reload the configuration at the start to identify the new squid service as follows:

```
# firewall-cmd --reload
# firewall-cmd --permanent --add-service=squid
# firewall-cmd --reload
```

Similarly, to update a specified zone other than the default zone, we will use the following commands:

```
# firewall-cmd --permanent --add-service=squid --zone=work
# firewall-cmd --reload
```

Should we later need to remove this service from the work zone, we can use the following command:

```
# firewall-cmd --permanent --remove-service=squid --zone=work
# firewall-cmd --reload
```

Firewall rules using ports

In the previous example, where the squid service only required a single port, we could easily add a port rule to allow access to a service. Although the process is simple, in some organizations, the preference will still be to create the service file that documents the need of the port in the description field.

If we need to add a port, we have similar options in `--add-port` and `--remove-port`. The following command shows how to add the squid TCP port `3128` to the work zone without the need to define the service file:

```
# firewall-cmd --permanent --add-port=3128/tcp --zone=work
# firewall-cmd --reload
```

Masquerading and Network Address Translation

If your `firewalld` server is your network router running RHEL 7, you may wish to provide access to the Internet to your internal hosts on a private network. If this is the case, we can enable masquerading. This is also known as **NAT (Network Address Translation)**, where the server's public IP address is used by internal clients. To establish this, we can make use of the built-in internal and external zones and configure masquerading on the external zone. The internal NIC should be assigned to the internal zone and the external NIC should be assigned to the external zone.

To establish masquerading on the external zone, we can use the following command:

```
# firewall-cmd --zone=external --add-masquerade
```

Masquerading is removed using the `--remove-masquerade` option. We may also query the status of masquerading in a zone using the `--query-masquerade` option. In the following screenshot, we can see masquerading being enabled and then queried with the resulting `yes` output:

```
[root@redhat7 ~]# firewall-cmd --zone=external --add-masquerade
success
[root@redhat7 ~]# firewall-cmd --zone=external --query-masquerade
yes
[root@redhat7 ~]# █
```

Using rich rules

The `firewalld` rich language allows an administrator to easily configure more complex firewall rules without having knowledge of the `iptables` syntax. This can include logging and examination of the source address.

To add a rule to allow NTP connection on the default zone, but logging the connection at no more than 1 per minute, use the following command:

```
# firewall-cmd --permanent \
--add-rich-rule='rule service name="ntp" audit limit value="1/m" accept'
# firewall-cmd --reload
```

Similarly, we can add a rule that only allows access to the squid service from one subnet only:

```
# firewall-cmd --permanent \
--add-rich-rule='rule family="ipv4" \
source address="192.166.0.0/24" service name="squid" accept'
# firewall-cmd --reload
```

From the following screenshot, we can see the rich rule being added:

```
[root@redhat7 ~]# firewall-cmd --permanent --add-rich-rule='rule family="ipv4" source address="19
2.166.0.0/24" service name="squid" accept'
success
[root@redhat7 ~]#
```

> The Fedora project maintains the documentation for rich rules in `firewalld` and these can be accessed at https://fedoraproject.org/wiki/Features/FirewalldRichLanguage should you need more detailed examples.

Implementing direct rules

If you have a prior experience with `iptables` and want to combine you knowledge of `iptables` with the features in `firewalld`, direct rules are here to help with this migration. Firstly, if we want to implement a rule on the INPUT chain, we can check the current settings with the following command:

```
# firewall-cmd --direct --get-rules ipv4 filter INPUT
```

If you have not added any rules, the output will be empty. We will add a new rule and use a priority of 0. This means that it will be listed at the top of the chain; however, this means little when no other rules are in place. We do need to verify that rules are added in the correct order to process if other rules are implemented:

```
# firewall-cmd --permanent --direct --add-rule ipv4 filter \
INPUT 0 -p tcp --dport 3128 -j ACCEPT
# firewall-cmd --reload
```

Reverting to iptables

Additionally, there is nothing stopping you from using the iptables service if this is what you are most familiar with.

Firstly, we can install iptables with the following command:

```
# yum install iptables-service
```

We can mask the firewalld service to more effectively disable the service, preventing it from being started without first unmasking this service:

```
# systemctl mask firewalld
```

We can enable iptables with the following commands:

```
# systemctl enable iptables
# systemctl enable ip6tables
# systemctl start iptables
# systemctl start ip6tables
```

Permanent rules are added as they always have been, via the /etc/sysconfig directory and the iptables and ip6tables files.

Summary

The `firewalld` project is maintained by Fedora and is the new administrative service and interface for the `netfilter` firewall on the Linux Kernel. As administrators, we can choose to use this default service or switch back to `iptables`; however, `firewalld` is able to provide us with the ability to reload configuration without dropping connections and mechanisms to migrate from `iptables`. We have seen how we can use zones to segregate network interfaces and sources if we need to share address ranges on a single NIC. Neither the NIC nor the source is bound to the zone. We can then add rules to a zone to control access to our resources. These rules are based on services or ports. If more complexity is required, we have the option of using rich or direct rules. Rich rules are written in the rich language from `firewalld`, whereas direct rules are written in the `iptables` syntax.

Index

O

Oracle VirtualBox
 URL 92
OU (Organizational Unit) 136

P

**PAM (Pluggable Authentication
 Modules)**
 about 11
 configuring 143
permissive domains 174
physical volume
 creating 59
PID (process ID) 176
policy type, SELinux
 minimum 166
 multi-level security (MLS) 166
 targeted 166
port-based virtual hosting 158
ports
 used, for firewall rules 183
privileges
 elevating 10
PTP
 implementing, on RHEL 7 48-52

R

**RAID (Redundant Array of Inexpensive
 Disks) 72, 80-82**
realm
 used, for managing domain
  enrolment 130-132
Red Hat
 NetworkManager 23, 24
Red Hat Enterprise Linux (RHEL) 1, 2
restorecon command 170
RHEL 7
 chronyd, implementing 44-47
 e-mail delivery, implementing 52, 53
 hostname configuring, hostnamectl
  used 21-23
 logging on to, Active Directory credentials
  used 132, 133
 ntpd, implementing 47, 48

 PTP, implementing 48-52
 Samba client 121, 122
 time services, configuring 43
routing 177

S

Samba client
 on RHEL 7 121, 122
Samba services
 about 114
 file shares, configuring 123, 124
 managing 117-121
 troubleshooting 124, 125
SELinux
 about 161, 162
 labels 164, 165
 modes 162
 policy 167
 policy type 166
 tools 169
 troubleshooting 172
SELinux, troubleshooting
 audit2allow command 173, 174
 log file 172, 173
 permissive domains 174
SIDs (Security Identifiers) 120
SMTP (Simple Mail Transfer Protocol) 52
snapper
 used, for managing snapshots 86-88
snapshots, btrfs
 about 82-85
 managing, snapper used 86-88
source
 managing 180
sssd
 Active Directory, using as identity
  provider 139, 140
 configuring 145
Start Of Authority (SOA) 39
static ports
 using, for NFSv3 108, 109
Storage Area Network (SAN) 57
su command
 about 10, 11
 su -l 10